29 Angel Patterns for Carvers

Al Streetman

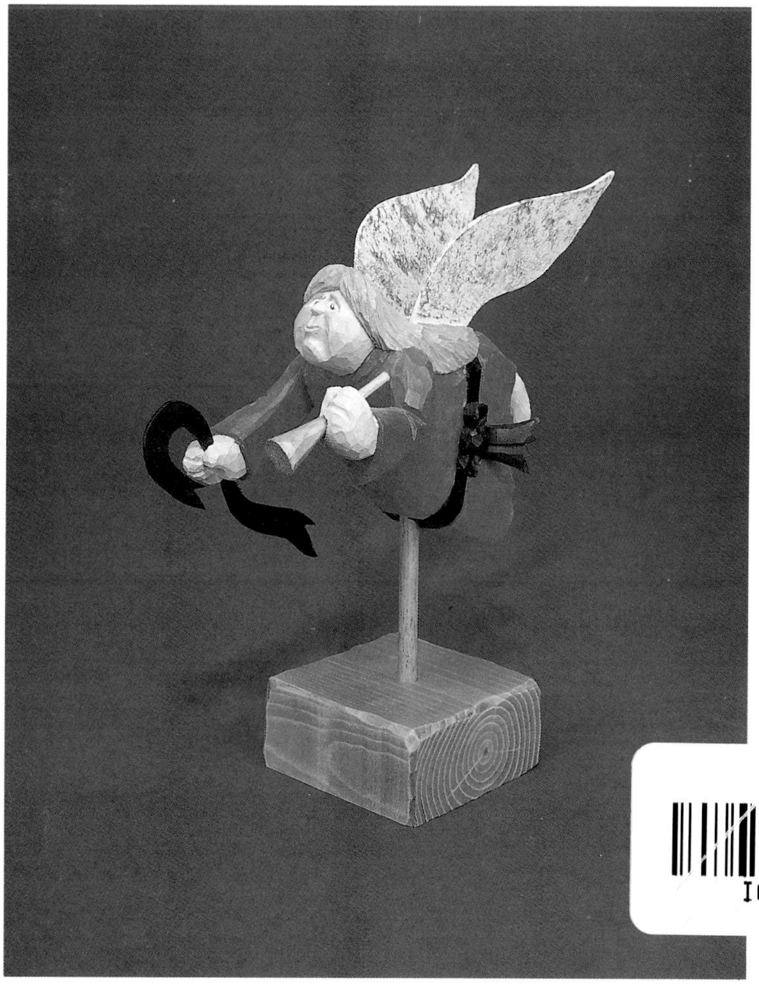

Schiffer Publishing Ltd
77 Lower Valley Road, Atglen, PA 19310

DEDICATION

To Grace Nicole, our newest "little angel"

ACKNOWLEDGMENTS

The following people helped make this book possible. I thank you all.

Marilynn Jones: For your continued word-processing support, both in data entry, and especially in data retrieval.

Jody Garrett, Woodcraft Supply Corp.: For all the help you give to us "starving artists", and for providing us with various carving tool samples for evaluation and consideration.

DecoArt: The paint samples were excellent, and satisfactory in all respects.

Woodcraft Supply Corp.; Parkersburg, WV.: Excellent carving tools and supplies.

Royal Brush Mfg., Inc.: Excellent quality paintbrushes at an affordable price.

CONTENTS

Introduction **3**
General Notes **4**
Carving Tools 4
Tips 4
General Painting Suggestions 6
Patterns **7**
The Project Pattern **32**
Carving the Project **33**
Painting the Project **56**
Antiquing &Assembling the Project **60**
Gallery & Study Models **62**

Library of Congress Catalog Card Number: 97-65109

ISBN: 0-7643-0275-2
Printed in China

Designed by Laurie A. Smucker

Published by Schiffer Publishing, Ltd.
77 Lower Valley Road
Atglen, PA 19310
Phone: (610) 593-1777
Fax: (610) 593-2002
E-mail:schifferbk@aol.com
Please write for a free catalog.
This book may be purchased from the publisher.
Please include $2.95 for shipping.
Try your bookstore first.

We are interested in hearing from
authors with book ideas on related subjects.

INTRODUCTION

Angels have been a constant source of mystery and fascination to us since time began. Although many of us have probably never seen an angel, we may have been influenced by one, and not even have realized it. The angel patterns in this book represent a "folk-art" approach to angel carving. These are the angels that came to mind and started appearing when I put pencil to paper. I have tried to make them simple enough in design that even a beginner could do them, yet when completed will make a nice addition to your carving collection. These angels are constructed using multiple parts, and will give you a new experience if you have never done carving of this type. The benefit of this method is that you ALWAYS get to take maximum advantage of the wood grain for the easiest carving, and you have much more freedom to pose your carvings in different attitudes and positions. This will help you eliminate the "stiffness" that is prevalent in many one-piece carvings. Once you learn this technique, you will discover ways to use it in making other carvings such as Santas, etc. For the carving project, we are going to carve an angel with a horn in one hand, a ribbon streaming from the other hand, and a bow on her robe. You will have a chance to learn easy ways to make ribbons and bows if you haven't tried them before. (The old bandsaw is going to be working overtime on this project!).

Each pattern in this book shows all the component pieces needed to make that particular angel. All the pieces are in scale to each other, so if you enlarge or reduce a pattern, the pattern pieces will still be in the right proportion to each other. If you desire a larger or smaller version, simply enlarge or shrink the pattern on a photocopying machine. (In the TIPS section, I explain reducing and enlarging patterns with a copying machine if this is new to you). You may also want to use the photocopying machine to make several sizes of the hand template. This way you will be sure to have a hand outline that is the proper size for the angel you carve.

The numbers on the arms of some of the patterns correspond to numbers on the hand template, and are the suggested hands to use for that pattern. If you would rather use different hands, feel free to do so. This will allow you to achieve many different looks from just a few patterns. Each pattern also shows an assembled view of the pieces, so you can picture how the completed angel might look if you desire to carve that pattern.

On the patterns, you will notice an arrow with a "G" superimposed over it. This arrow indicates the recommended grain direction of the wood in relation to the pattern, in order to make carving that particular piece as easy as possible.

I use Basswood whenever possible, but any soft wood such as Jelutong, clear Spruce, or Sugar/White Pine will work equally well. If possible, use a bandsaw with a 1/8" blade to cut out the pattern pieces. The bandsaw will allow you to release the rough version of the angel from the block of wood faster than trying to use a coping saw or other means to cut out the pattern. For making the major pattern pieces, the following recommendations are given. If you wish to use different wood dimensions regarding thickness, by all means feel free to do so:

BODY: 1-3/4" or 2" thick basswood

ARMS: 3/4" thick basswood

WINGS and FLOWING RIBBON: 1/16" or 1/8" thick hobby plywood (should be available at hobby or craft stores in your area)

HORNS, BOWS, HEARTS, etc.: Basswood of sufficient thickness to accommodate the pattern piece. This will vary, depending on which pattern you are carving.

WOODEN DOWEL: 5/16" in diameter, used to connect the angel to the mounting base.

SECTION OF 2" x 4" SCRAP WOOD: used as the base for the angel.

GENERAL NOTES

1. Trace the pattern pieces, or make a copy of them on a photocopying machine. Glue the pattern you copied or traced onto some heavy paper such as poster paper or a manila file folder. When the glue is dry, cut out the pattern. This method will prevent you from ruining the master patterns in your book.

2. Lay your pattern on the wood, trace the outline of it, and saw it out. **Pay close attention to any recommended grain directions indicated on the pattern pieces!!**

3. You should now have a rough blank ready to be carved.

4. Use your own techniques and style to bring the carving to the finished stage.

5. You will notice that some of the patterns do not show hands attached to some of the arms. (This is where you will put the hand template to work). Many times the type of hands will be determined by what accessories you are going to include with the carving. Because you are carving the hands separately from the body, you can orient them to take advantage of the wood grain when you saw them out. This will allow you endless variations of hand positions, so you can give more life to your carvings. Also, if you are creating an extreme caricature, you can use a larger than normal hand pattern to add more humor to the carving. In the TIPS section, there is information describing hand carving separately from the arm, if you are not familiar with this technique.

6. **I recommend that you read the entire book before starting the project**. This will help you see where we are going, and will help alert you to carving techniques that may be unfamiliar. In the section where we paint the angel, you may see an area or detail that might not have been clear to you in the carving section. Reading the entire book through before beginning the project will help you identify any such areas, and may help eliminate frustration at a later time. Remember, if we carve it, we will paint it, so you will see everything at least twice.

CARVING TOOLS

For those of you who may want to duplicate the cuts I make using the same tools as I use, I have listed below the tools used in my angel carvings.

1/8" V gouge - Hair details, seam separations

1/4" V gouge - Seam separations, hair details, wrinkles in clothes

2mm #11 U gouge - Large hair details, minor scooping

3mm #11 U gouge - Large hair details, minor scooping

5mm #3 Flat gouge - Wood removal in restricted areas

8mm #2 Flat gouge - Wood removal in large areas

10mm #7 U gouge - Scooping wood to simulate folds in the robes

4mm #8 U gouge - Scooping wood to simulate small folds

Fixed blade (Bütz) carving and detail knives - General wood removal and details such as eye carving.

TIPS

1. EYES

A. **QUILT PIN METHOD:** I often use various sizes of plastic-head quilting pins to make eyes. Mark where you want the eyes to be on the finished carving. Using a drill and bit that is slightly larger than the pin head you are going to use, make a hole for each eye.

Using wire cutters, snip off the pin head, leaving about 1/4" of the pin attached to the head.

Insert the pin head into the eye socket, with the pin end going in first. Use a nail set to seat the head into the hole until only a small orb protrudes. This gives a fairly realistic eye without causing too much effort on your part. For extra detail, remove a triangular-shaped piece of wood from the sides of the pin head. This will make a very realistic eye when it is painted.

B. **PUNCH METHOD:** A second way to create eyes the easy way is to use carver's eye punches. Select the size eye punch you want to use, based on the size of the eye sockets you have made. Push the eye punch against the socket firmly and rotate it. After making both eyes, remove triangular-shaped pieces of wood from the corners to give more detail. Use your knife, if necessary, to smooth and round off the eyeball.

C. **FOOTBALL METHOD:** A more realistic way to make eyes is to first of all carve the eye sockets so that about a 90° angle is formed. Lightly sketch in a football-shaped eye in each socket, such that the top half of the football is on the upper half of the socket, and the lower half of the football is on the lower half of the socket. When you sketch in the footballs, make the outside ends lower than the inside ends. Using the tip of your knife, score the football outline to a depth of about 1/16". Now use the tip of your knife to remove triangular-shaped pieces of wood from the left and right corner of each eye. This will leave a small section of wood inside each football, which will be the eyeball. Use your knife to round off and smooth the eyeball. You can vary the way you remove the triangular-shaped corners, if you want the eyes to be looking more to one side, rather than straight ahead.

D. **MOUND METHOD: The** most realistic way to make eyes is to first rough carve the nose so it is standing out from the face. Next, sketch a circle or oval on each side of the nose to represent where the eye mounds will be located. Using a smaller "V" gouge such as a 1/8" size, or your knife tip, go around the circles or ovals so the mounds will be defined, and separated from the face area. Use your knife to round the sharp edges of the mounds, and the face area around the mounds.

Divide the mounds into thirds by sketching two curved horizontal lines across each one, making sure that the lines join at each corner of the mound.(Look at your own eyes in a mirror to see what I mean here). Using your knife tip, score each horizontal line about 1/16" deep. Working from the center of the eye mound, use your knife tip to shave **upward** toward the top horizontal line, and **downward** toward the bottom horizontal line. This will make the eyelids stand out from the eyeball area. Finally, remove small triangular pieces of wood from each corner of the eye, so the eyeball will be rounded from left to right, as well as top to bottom.

Changing the size and shape of the mounds, and the spacing between the horizontal lines, will allow you to achieve many effects and expressions on your carvings.

One last thing concerning eyes: Don't get upset if you discover that you have carved one eye smaller or at a different angle than the other eye. This "accident" may work to your advantage. It will lend an interesting variation to the carving, and no one has to know you didn't do it that way on purpose!!

2. BUYING WOOD

When buying wood, whether it be Basswood, Spruce, or some other type, try to pick the **lightest** pieces. They tend to have less fat and sap in them, so they are **easier** to carve.

3. WRINKLES & FOLDS

An easy way to help determine where you want to place some wrinkles and folds in the arms, torso and legs is to observe and note where the wood grain changes direction as you are carving. Usually in the crook of an elbow or behind the knees, you will notice that wood "fuzzies" try to appear, no matter how carefully you carve or how sharp your knife is. That is because the wood grain direction is changing, and in one direction or the other, you are trying to carve against the grain, thus the "fuzzies" appear. These spots are perfect candidates for wrinkles and folds, made with a large "V" tool or by cutting wedges out with your knife. As a beginning carver, if you do nothing more than add a few cuts in these areas, you will be amazed at the difference in the way the carving looks. With experience, you will start noticing other places to add wrinkles and folds.

4. ENLARGING AND REDUCING PATTERNS

For those of you who have never had much practice enlarging or reducing patterns, or being able to calculate how much enlargement or reduction you need to select on the photocopying machine, here are some general guidelines:

Let's say you have a pattern that shows a side profile requiring 2" thick wood, and you want to make the pattern larger so it will fit on 3" thick wood. Use the following formula to calculate what percentage enlargement to select on the copier:

[New Dimension Desired ÷ Present Dimension] x 100 =
% to select on copier machine.

Using our example, this would work out as follows:

[3" ÷ 2"] x 100 = 150%

Going the other way, let's say you have a pattern that shows a 2" side profile, and you want to reduce it down so it will fit on a piece of 1-3/4" thick wood. Using the same formula, it works out as follows:

[1.75" ÷ 2"] x 100 = **87.5 %** .

If the machine you are using won't cut large enough or small enough to get the job done on the first try, additional steps may be required. Go ahead and make your first copy using the largest enlargement or reduction setting you can select. Measure the **new** dimensions on your copy, **(which will now be your Present Dimension)**, then use the same formula as before to calculate how much additional enlargement or reduction is needed to get the pattern to the size you desired it to be.

5. HANDS

When making separate hands that are going to be holding some object such as a ribbon, it is easiest if you first cut out the top profile of the hand, drill a hole large enough for the object to fit through, then saw out the side profile of the hand. This procedure will help prevent the hand from splitting when you drill it.

For those patterns where the hands are to be carved separately, the following instructions may be used if you are not familiar with this method of hand carving:

(A) Lay out the top view of the hands on a piece of 3/4" thick basswood. Leave a short section of wood at the rear of each hand when you lay out the pattern.

This section will serve as a handle while you carve and shape the hands, and will form the wrist pegs in a later step. Saw out the top profile of the hands.

(B) Now, using the top set of hands in the Hand Studies as a reference, sketch in the side profile of the hands, then saw them out. You now should have two hands that will require very little work to finish.

(C) Sketch in the thumbs. Remove wood from each hand using a knife or a **#7 10mm "U" gouge**, so the thumbs are well-defined, then round off the sharp edges of the thumbs.

(D) Draw a line in the middle of the finger section to divide it in half. Now draw lines to divide each of these sections in half. You should now have four fingers defined, all approximately equal.

(E) Using a **1/8" "V" gouge**, go over these lines so the fingers will be separated. *As an option*, to add further detail without too much pain on your part, use a bandsaw, scroll saw or coping saw to carefully saw along these lines. Use your knife to remove any fuzzy wood caused by the saw cuts, and to remove any sharp edges still remaining on the hands. At this point, if you do nothing else, you will have two hands that will look perfectly good once they are painted. Experienced carvers may add more detailing as they desire, such as knuckles and wrinkles on the finger joints.

F) Using your knife, trim down the sections of wood protruding from the rear of the hands, so as to form a "wrist" or "pin" that will fit snugly into the holes you drilled earlier in the arms. When done properly, the hand should appear to be coming out of the sleeve. This method allows you to turn the hands in various directions, so your carvings will appear more lifelike.

GENERAL PAINTING SUGGESTIONS FOR ALL ANGELS IN THIS BOOK

I have included some *suggested* colors and paint brushes for all patterns. If you have a preference for a different color scheme, by all means use it. After all, it's your angel, and you can dress them any way you desire.

I have also listed the colors produced by DecoArt and their identification numbers, which I have found to be suitable for painting these carvings. I have used these colors, and the results were excellent. I hope this will help minimize your confusion when trying to sort through the maze of paint brands and colors at your hobby or craft store.

The best paintbrushes I have found, for the money, are made by the Royal Brush Mfg. Company. They come in a wide assortment of sizes and shapes, are durable, and most important are affordable. In general, here are the ones I use and recommend for painting your carvings. All brushes are Golden Taklon® series:

Details such as eyes, other small areas: **Series 250**, #0 and #00
Large areas: **Series 170**, #2 and #4
Details in large areas: **Series 180**, #6
Blending: **Series 150**, #2, #4
Series 250 are round detail brushes
Series 170 are Cat Tongues (Filberts)
Series 180 are Triangular
Series 150 are Flat Shaders

You may have heard and read this a million times, but when painting your carvings, keep the word **THIN** in mind. What you want to do is stain the wood to give it some color and life, but you don't want the paint so thick that it covers up the beauty of the wood. **NOTE:** When painting the head and hands, I generally use a little thicker mixture of paint than I use on the rest of the carving. I want the face to be a bit more intense than the rest of the carving, since the head and face is what sets most of the mood for the carving.

Titanium White #DA1 - Eyes, highlight in eyes
Buttermilk #DA3 - Wings
Lamp (Ebony) Black #DA67 - Eye dots, slippers on feet
Fleshtone #DA78 - Face, hands, other skin areas
Baby Blue #DA42 - Eye dots
Blush Flesh #DA110 - "Blushing" on cheeks and around mouth area
Berry Red #DA19 - Ribbons, bows
Prussian Blue #DA138 - Ribbons, bows
Venetian Gold #DA72 - Horns

SUGGESTED HAIR and EYEBROW COLORS:

Cadmium Yellow #DA10
Antique Gold #DA146
Sable Brown #DA61
Dark Chocolate #DA65

SUGGESTED ROBE COLORS:

Lavender #DA34
Plum #DA175
Boysenberry Pink #DA29
Santa Red #DA170
Yellow Green #DA134
Williamsburg Blue #DA40
True Blue #DA36
Sapphire #DA99
Oak Antiquing Gel #DS30 - "Aging" the finished carving
Clear Satin Varnish #DS15 - Sealing the finished carving

Remember: These are only a few of the many colors you can use for your angels. Should you have other color preferences, use them. Don't be afraid to get wild and experiment with all sorts of color combinations. For those of you (like me), who have difficulty trying to decide which colors work well together, most hobby and art supply stores sell inexpensive color wheels which will show you colors that work together, and colors that oppose each other. I have listed a few combinations here, for illustrative purposes:

MAIN COLOR	CONTRAST COLOR
Red	Green
Orange	Blue
Yellow	Violet

A good color wheel will not only show you main and contrast colors, it will also show colors that blend.

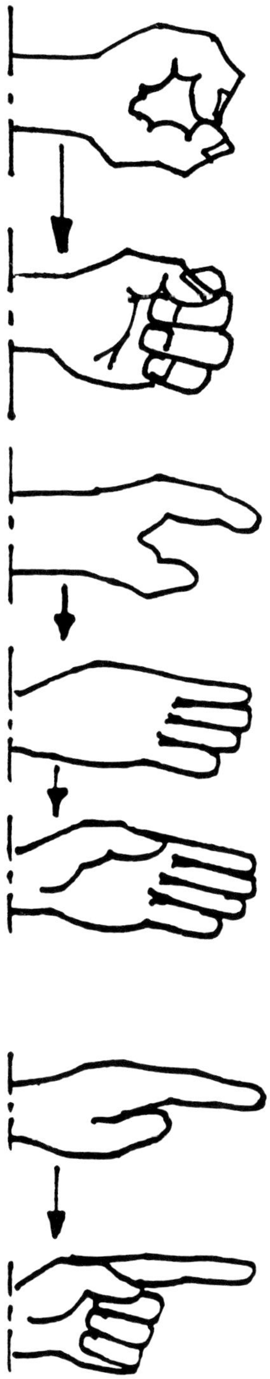

HAND STUDIES

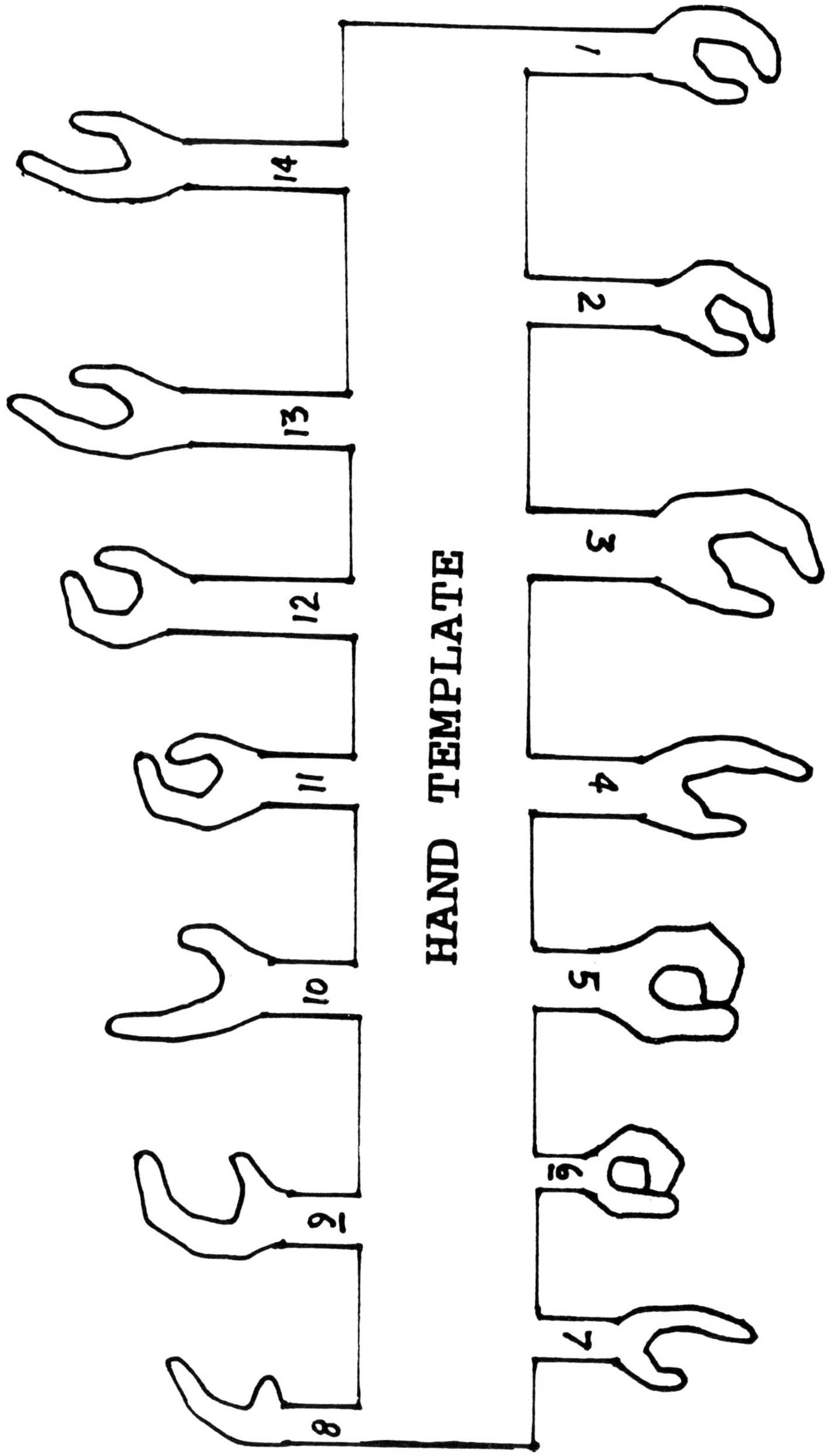

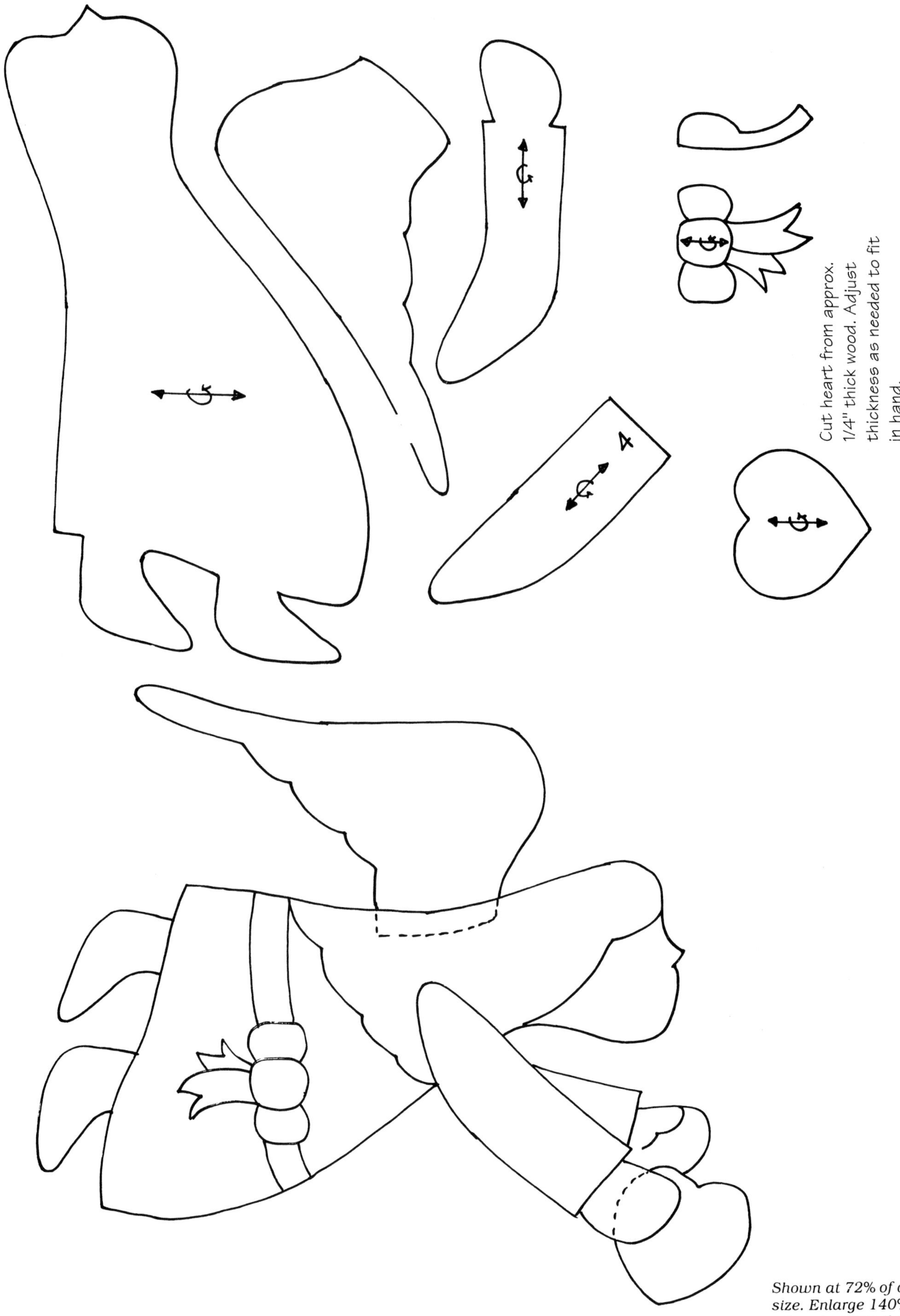

Shown at 72% of original size. Enlarge 140% to return to original size.

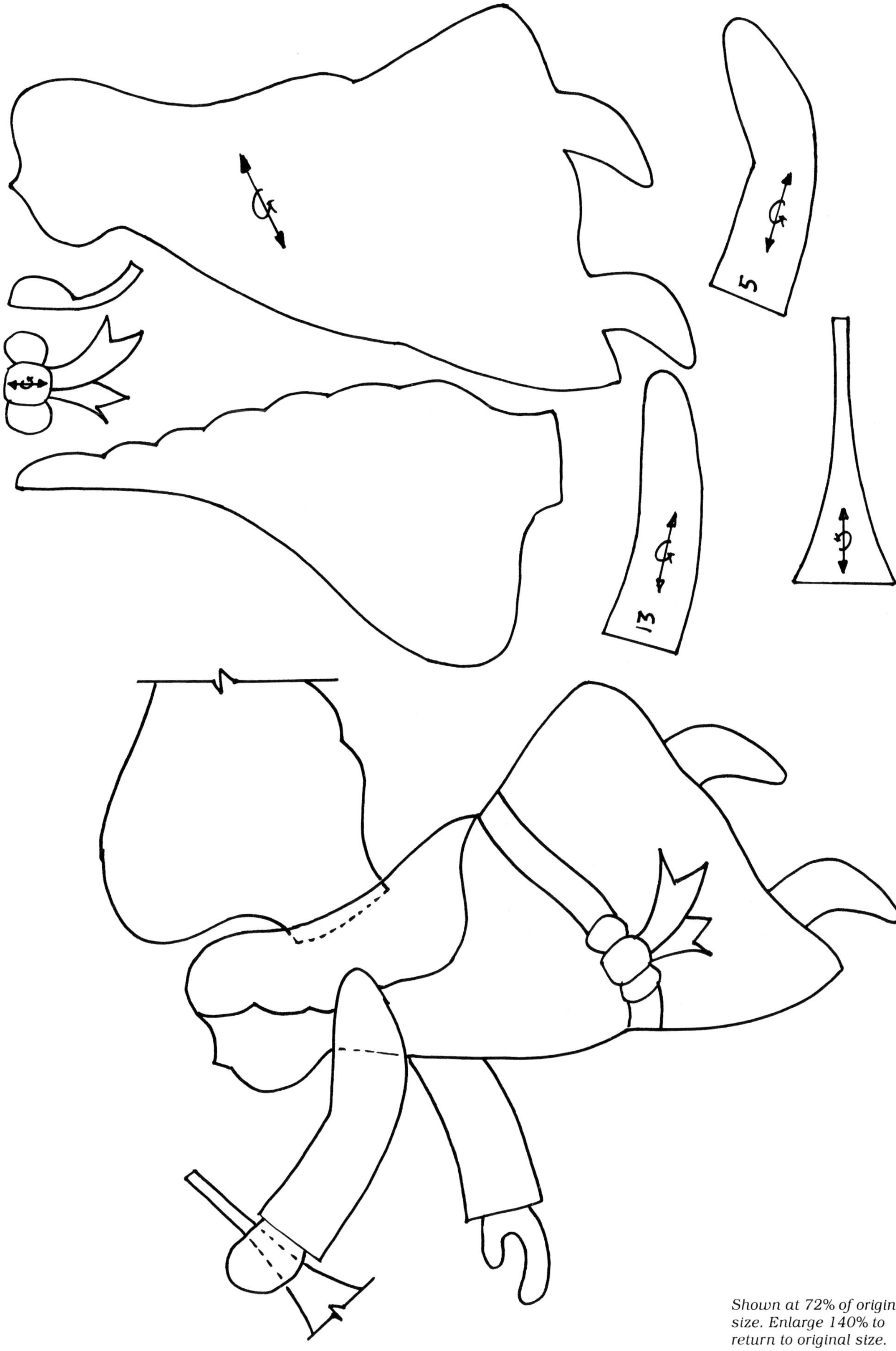

Shown at 72% of original size. Enlarge 140% to return to original size.

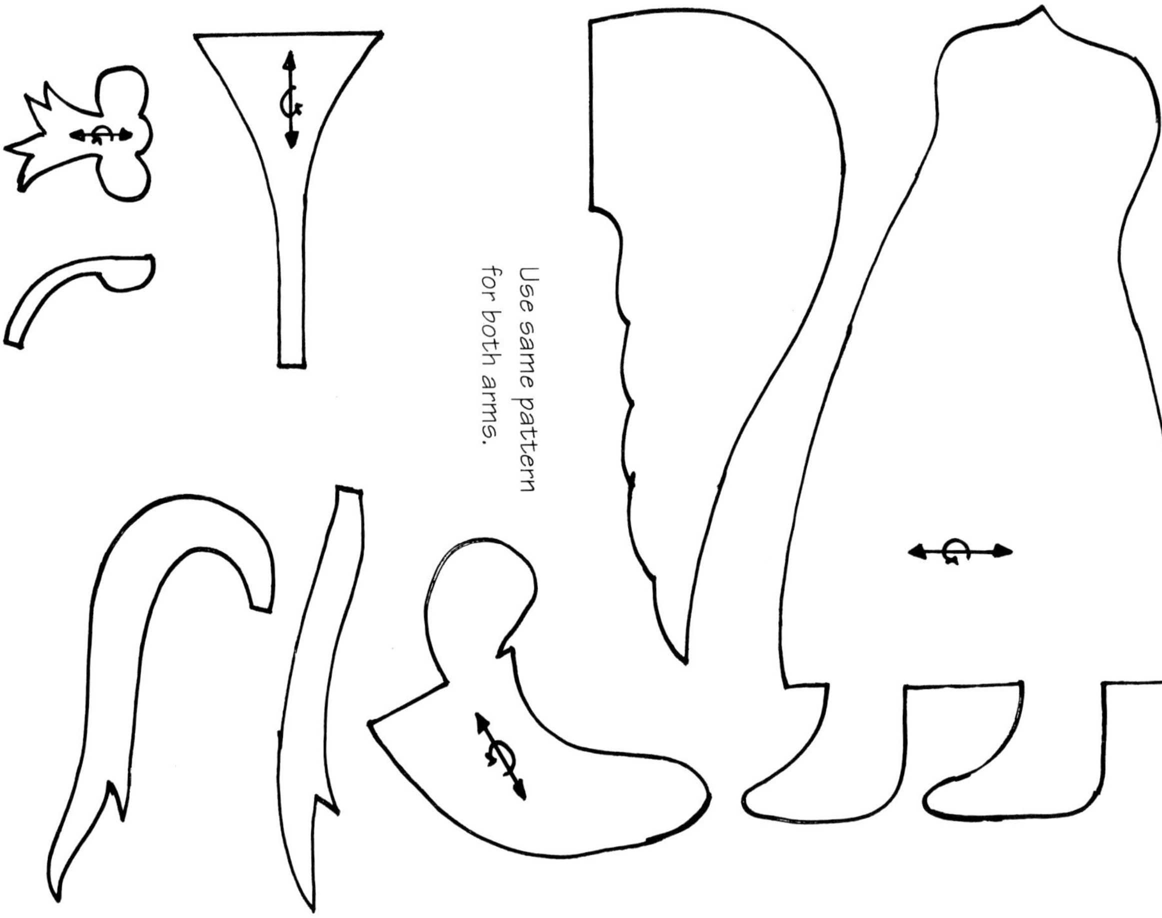

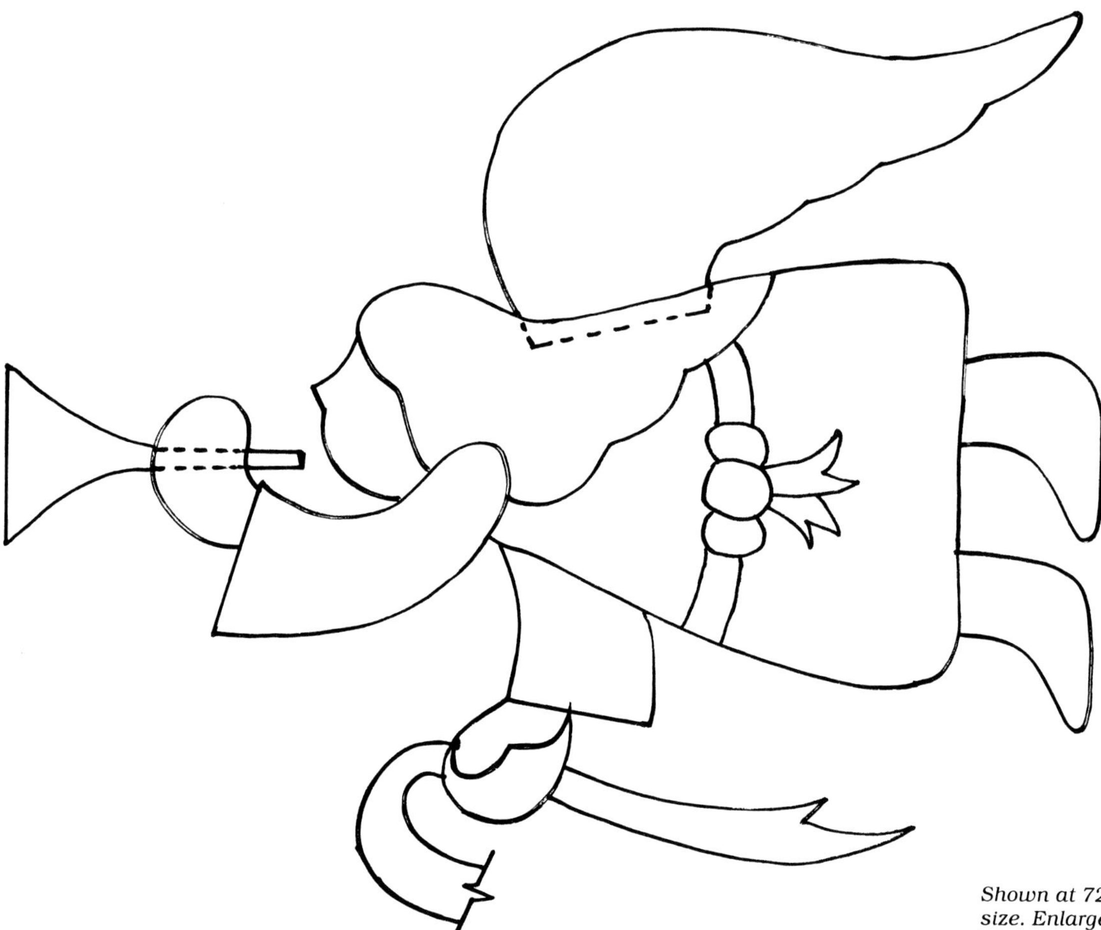

Shown at 72% of original size. Enlarge 140% to return to original size.

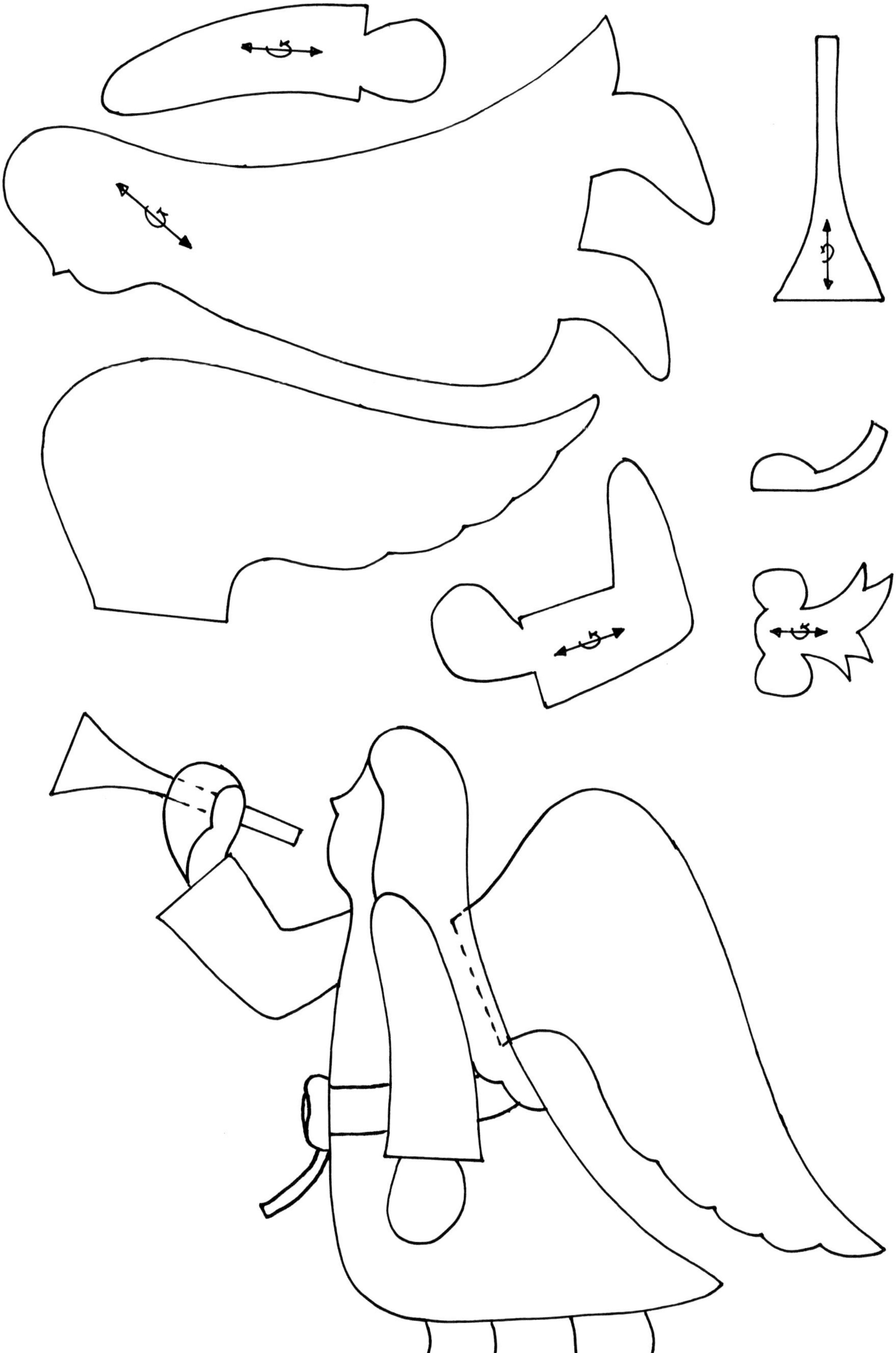

Shown at 72% of original size. Enlarge 140% to return to original size.

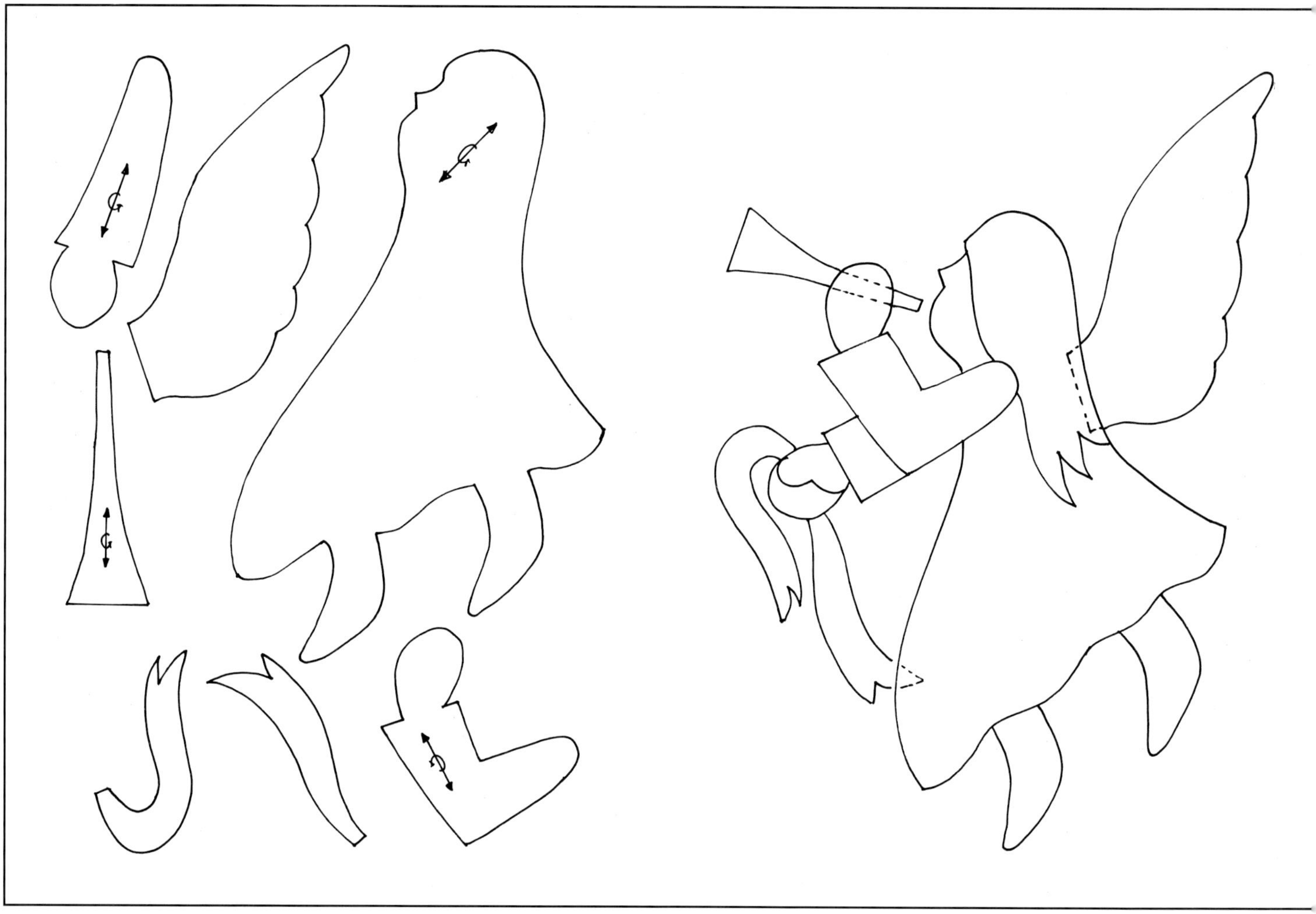

Shown at 50% of original size. Enlarge 200% to return to original size.

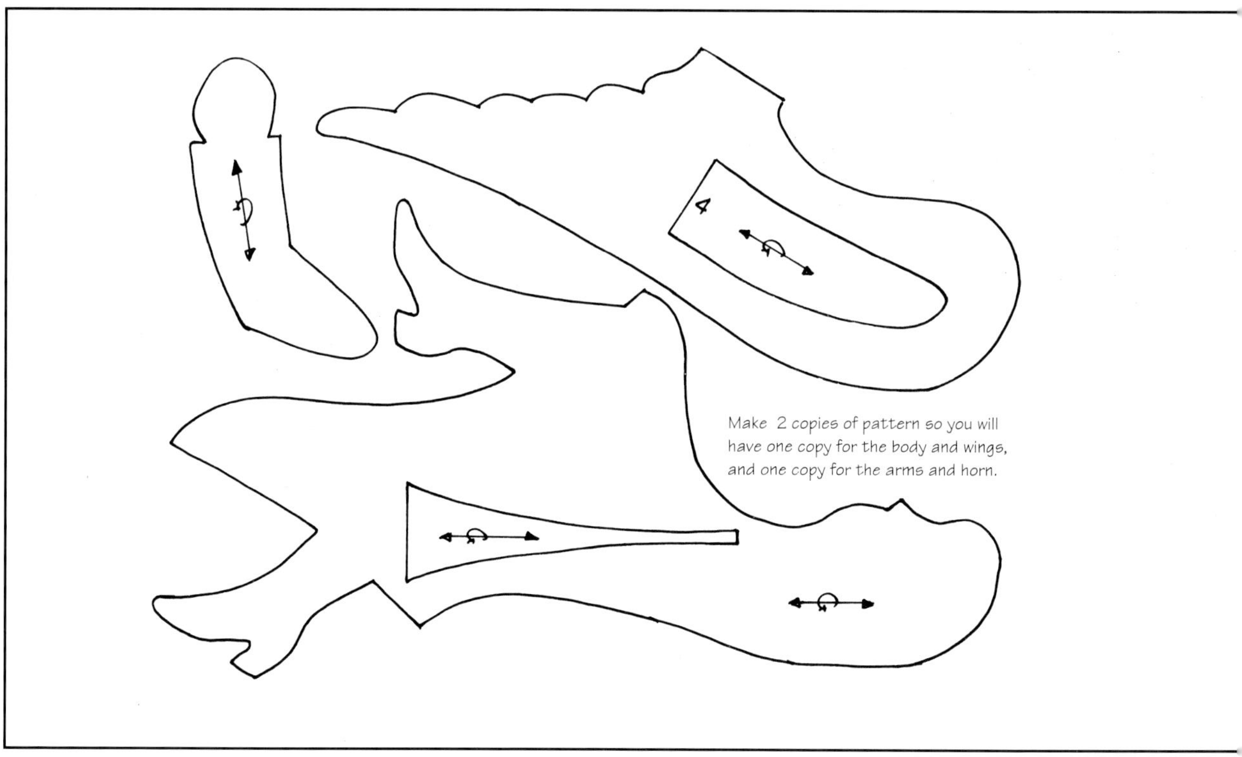

Make 2 copies of pattern so you will have one copy for the body and wings, and one copy for the arms and horn.

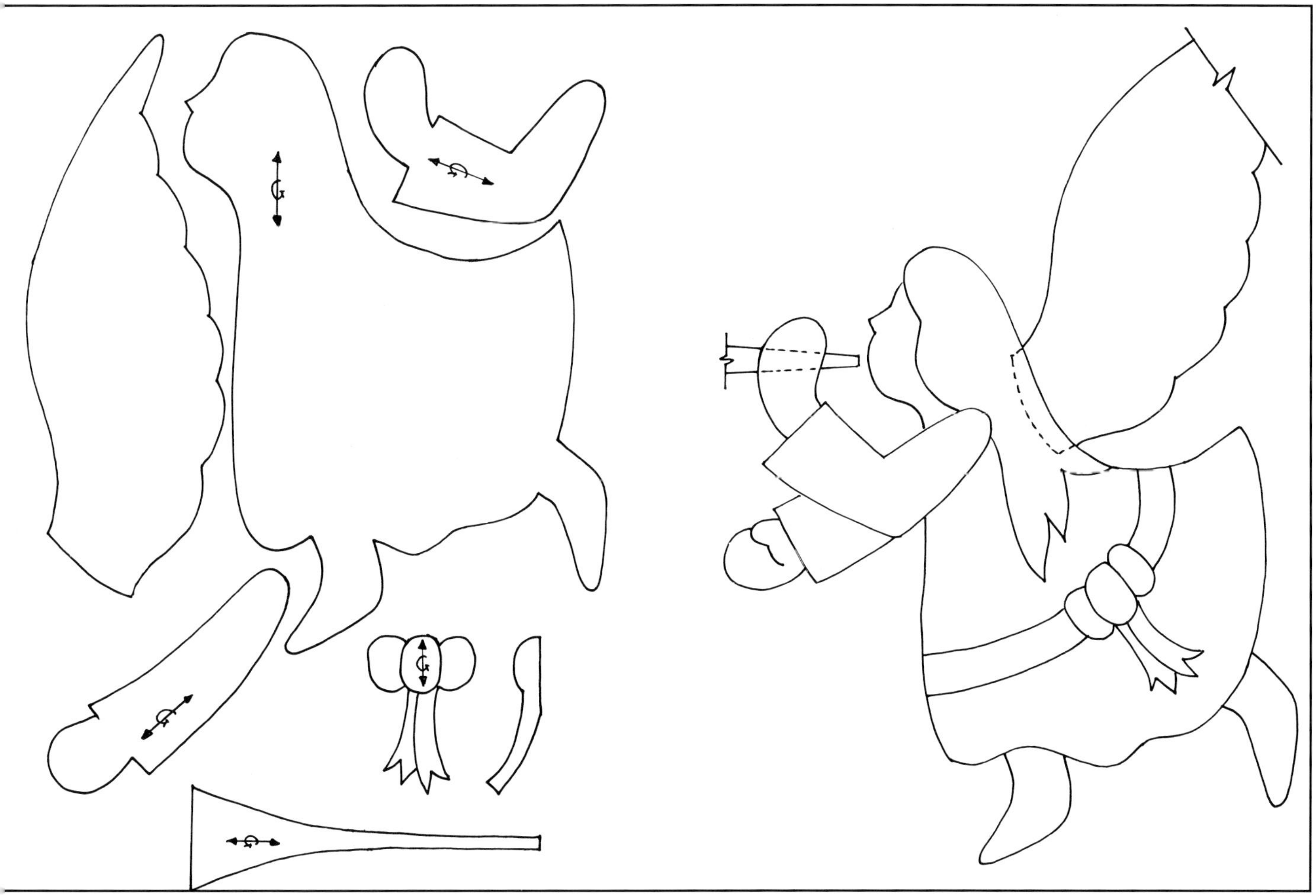

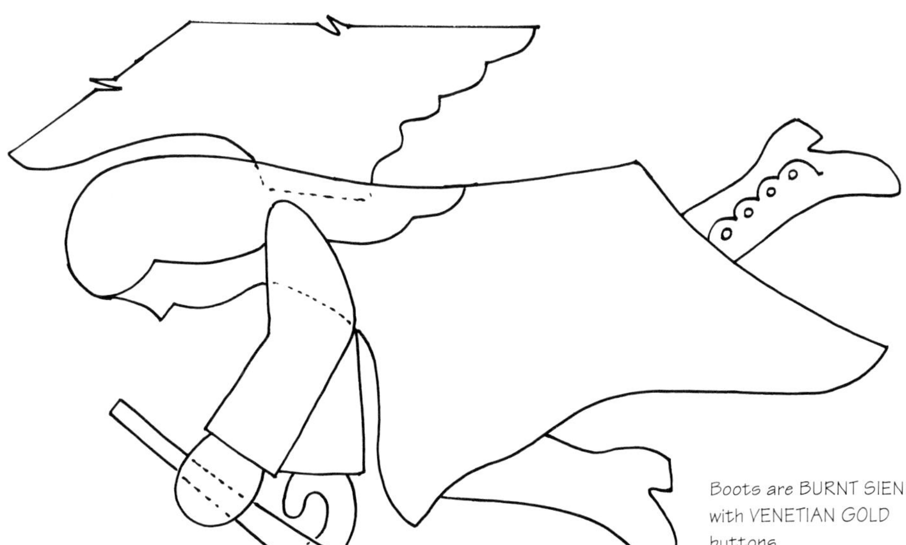

Boots are BURNT SIENNA with VENETIAN GOLD buttons.

Carve boot details using a knife or gouge. Buttons on boots are made with a 1/8" eye punch.

Shown at 50% of original size. Enlarge 200% to return to original size.

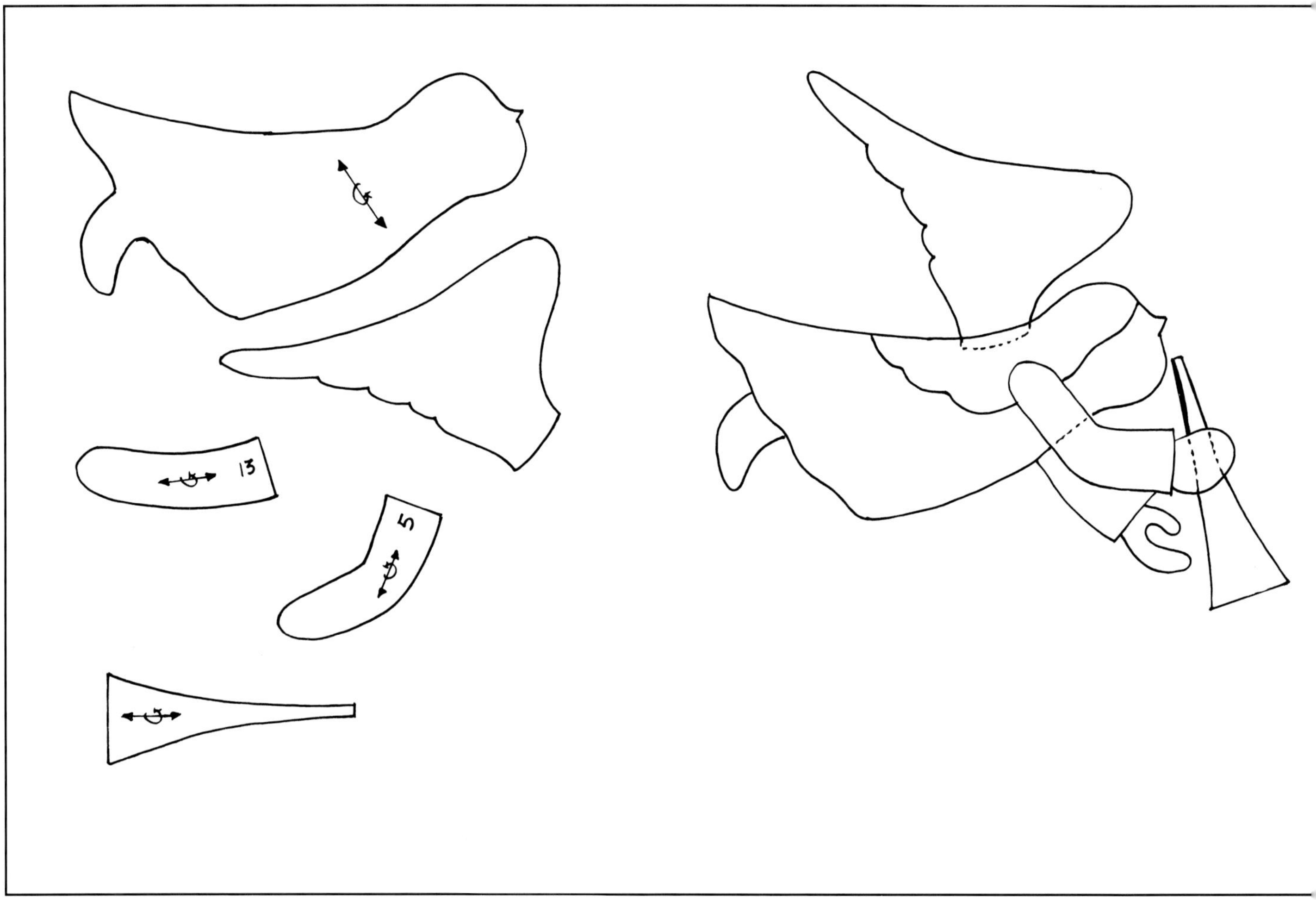

Shown at 50% of original size. Enlarge 200% to return to original size.

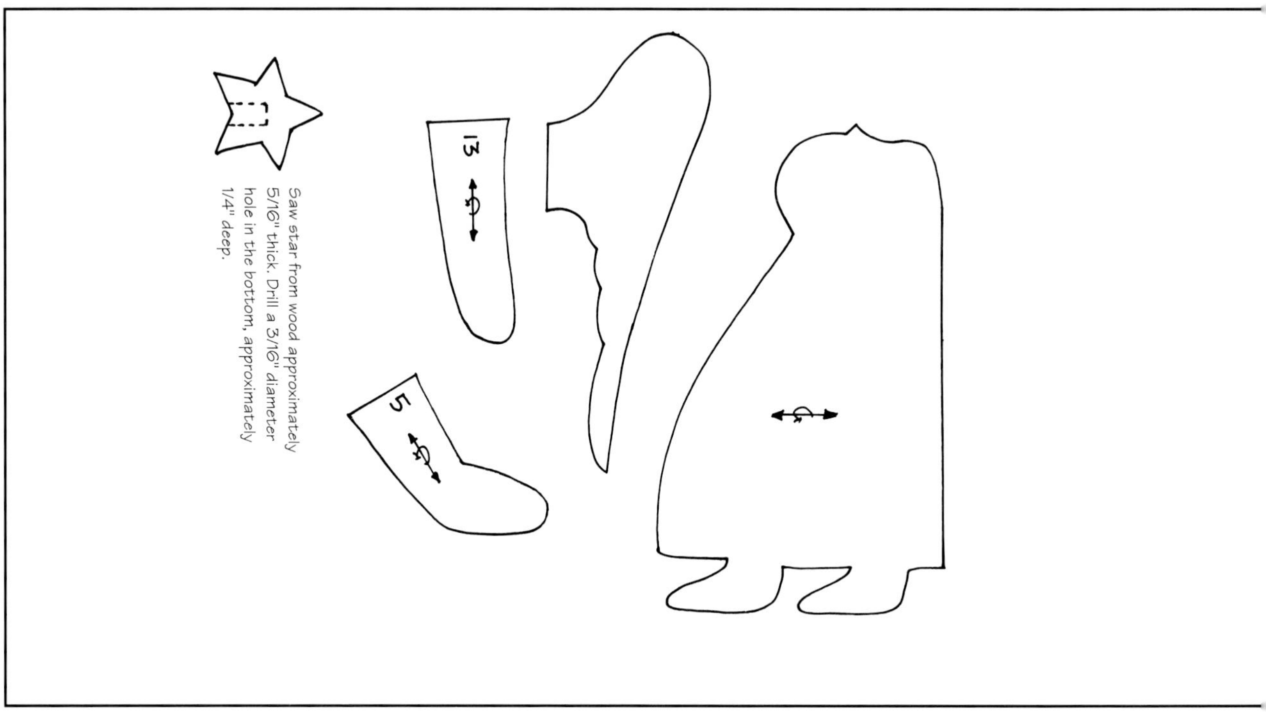

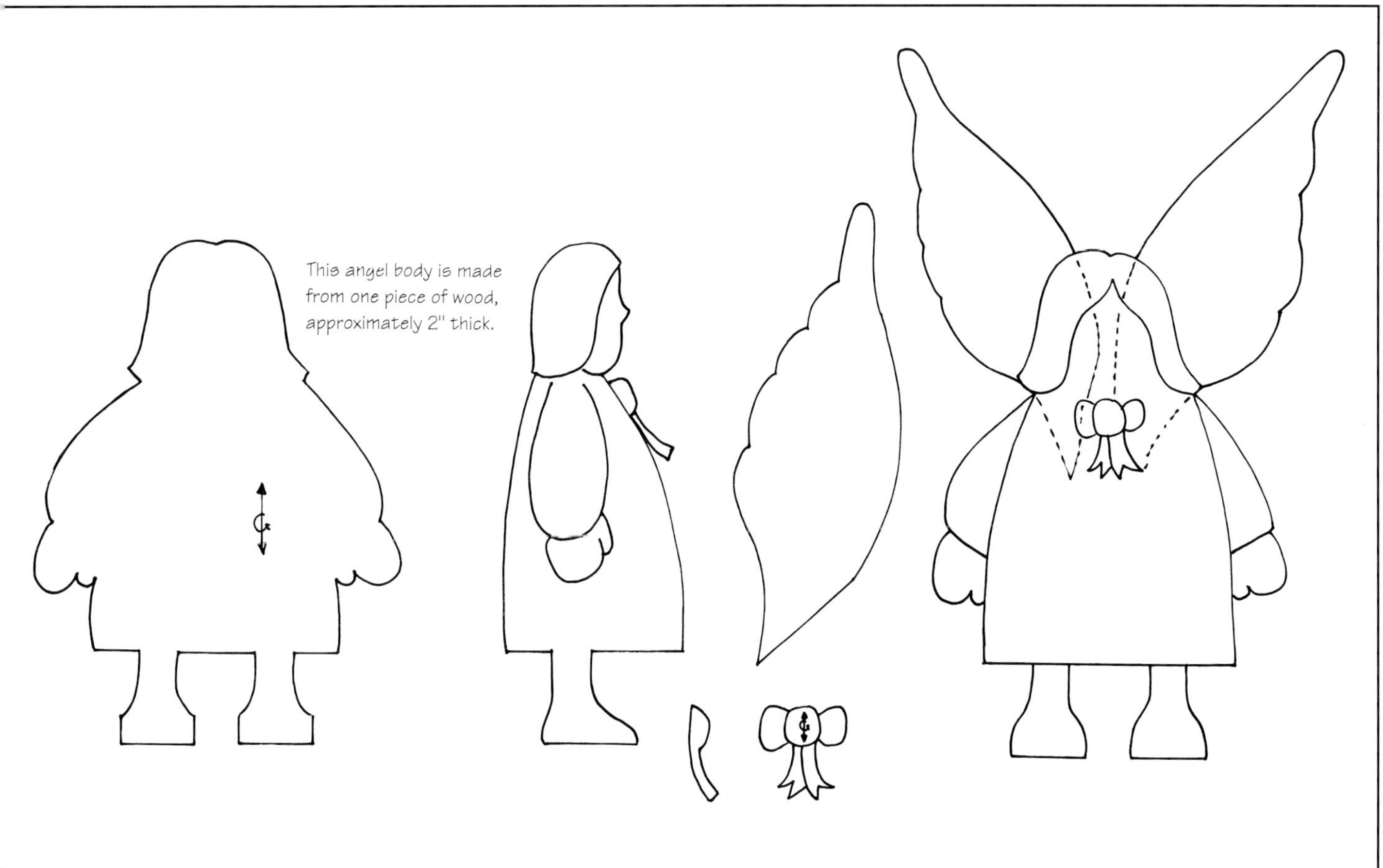

Shown at 50% of original size. Enlarge 200% to return to original size.

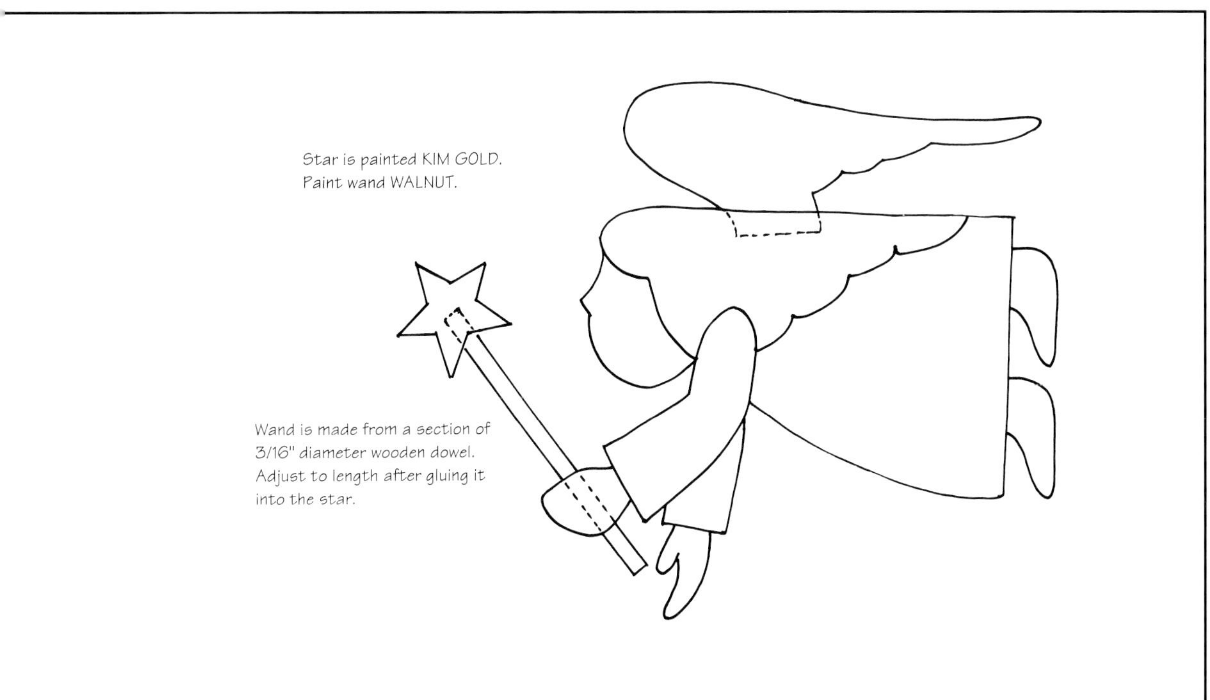

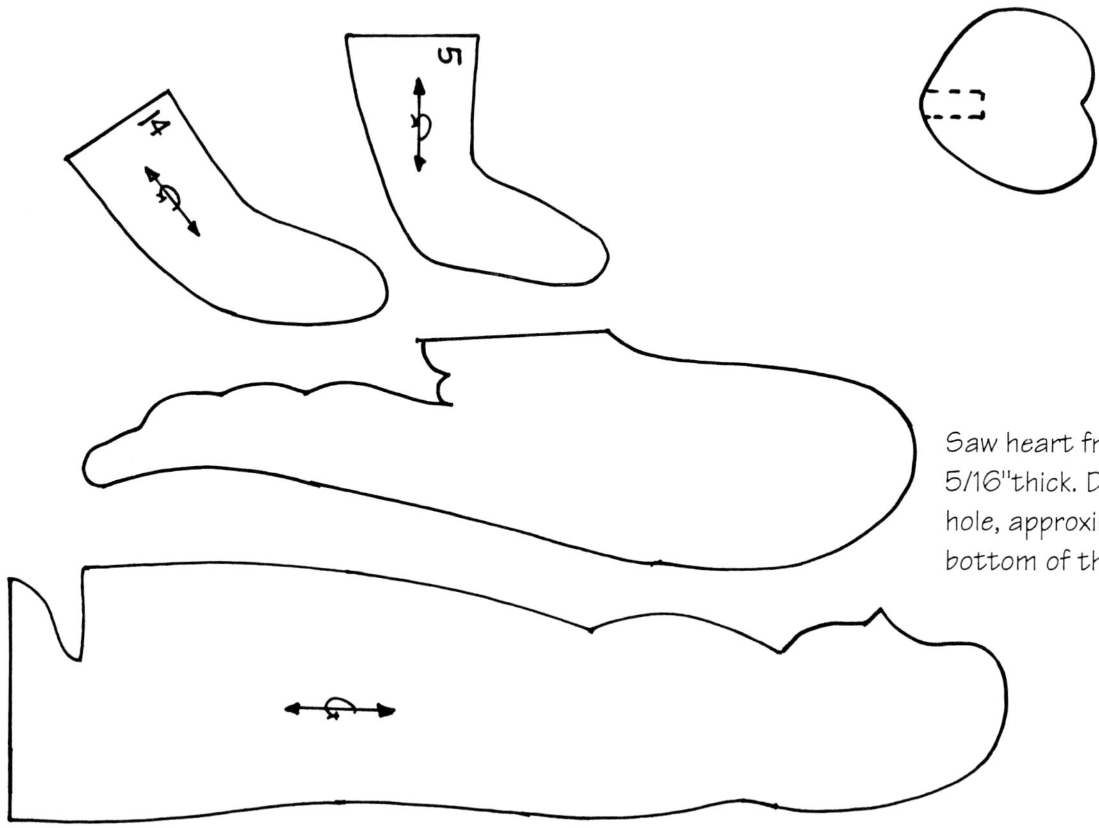

Saw heart from wood approximately 5/16"thick. Drill a 3/16" diameter hole, approximately 1/4" deep in the bottom of the heart.

Staff is made from a section of 3/16" diameter wooden dowel. Adjust to length after gluing it to the heart.

Paint staff RAW UMBER.

Shown at 72% of original size. Enlarge 140% to return to original size.

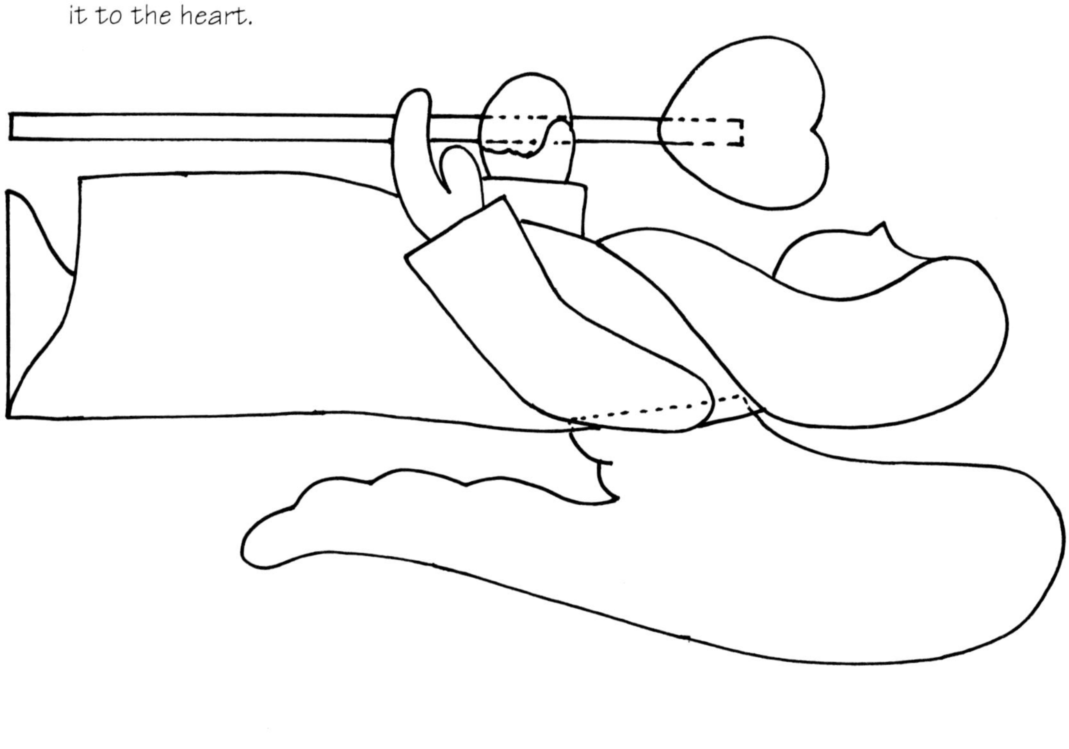

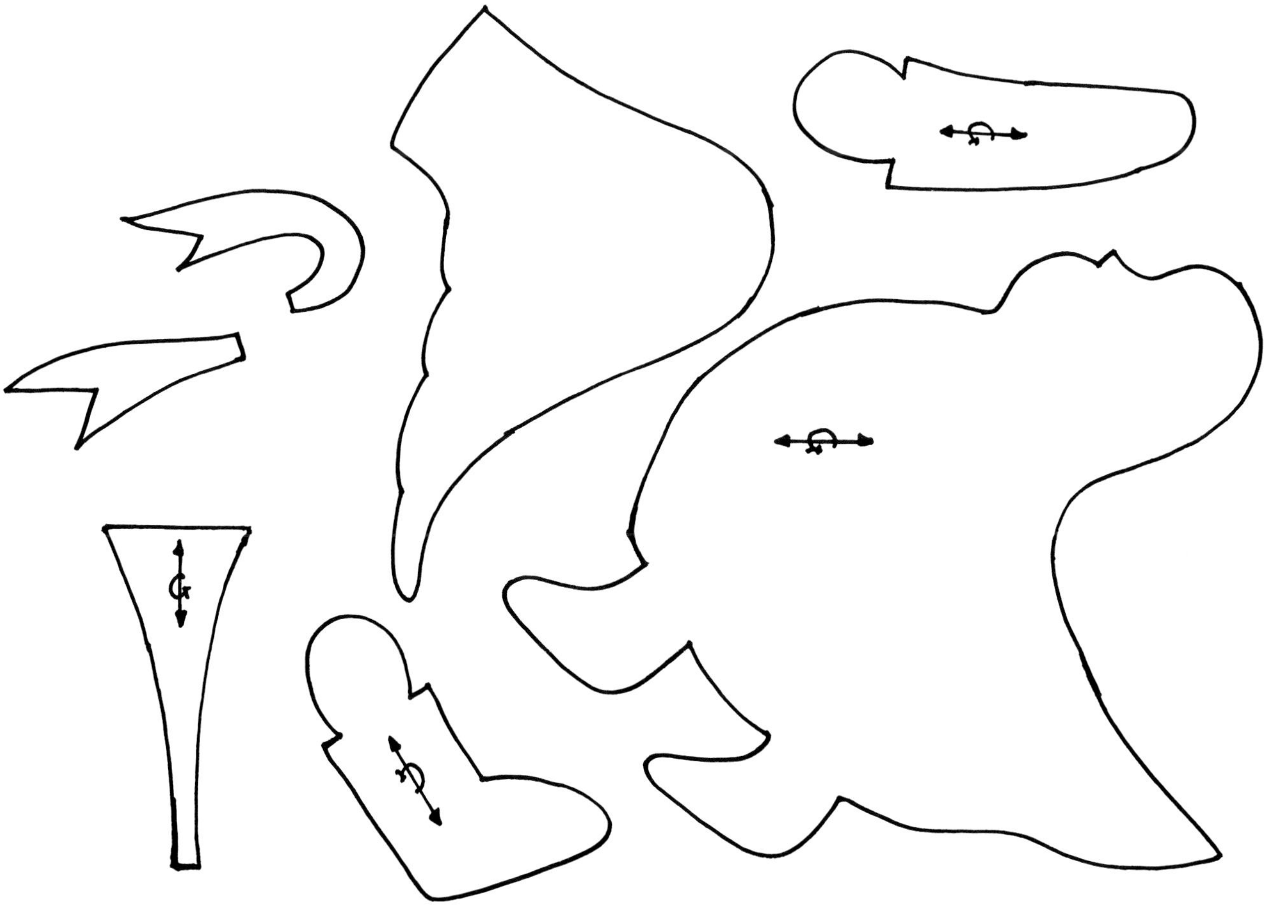

Shown at 72% of original size. Enlarge 140% to return to original size.

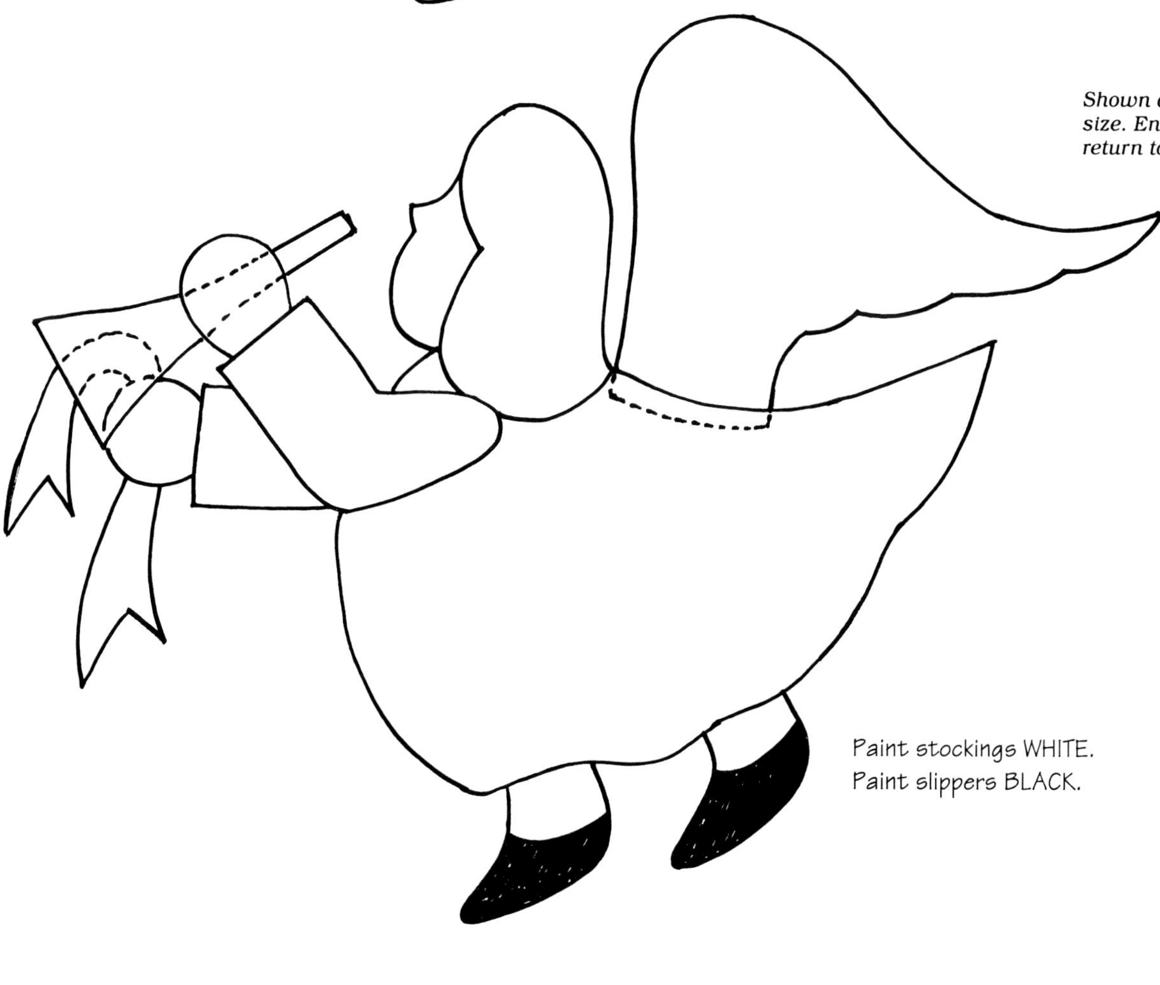

Paint stockings WHITE.
Paint slippers BLACK.

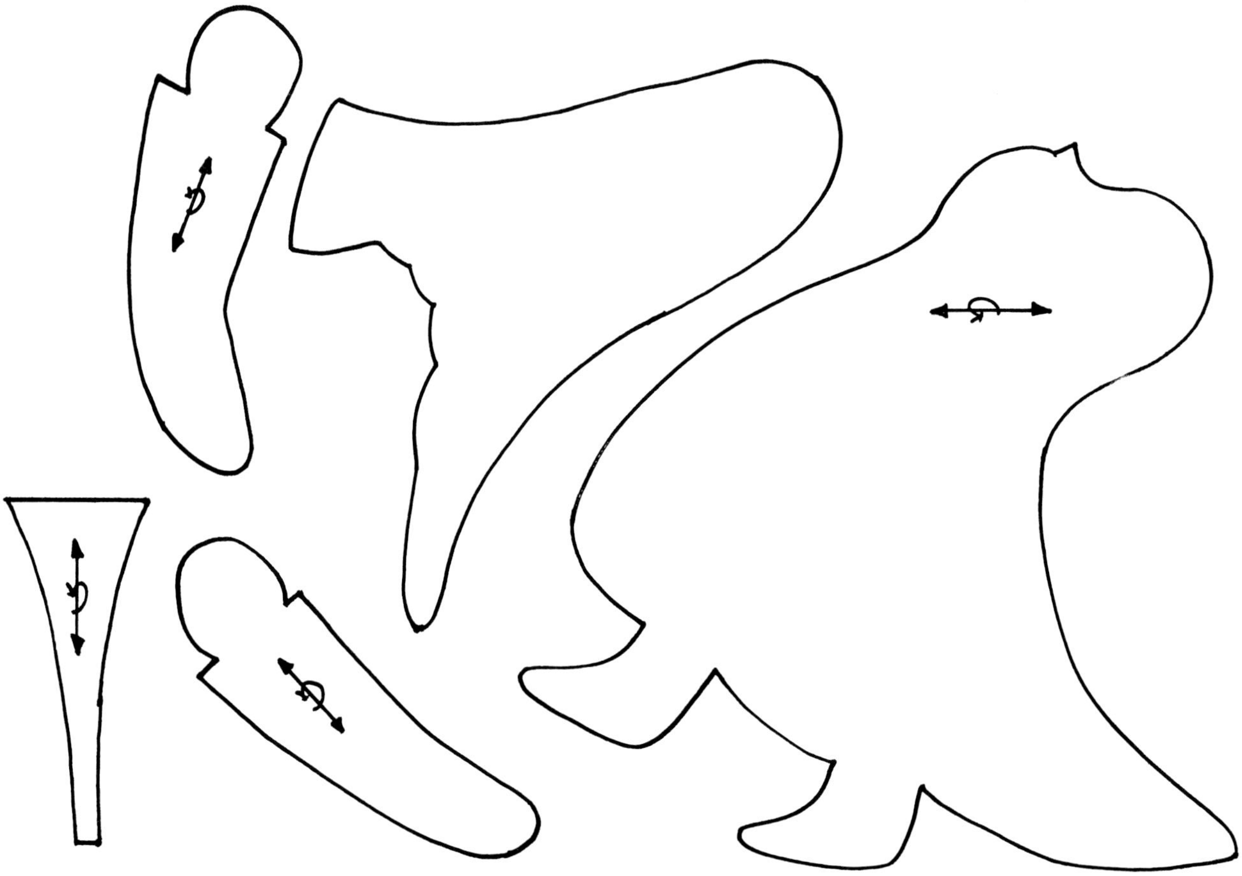

Shown at 72% of original size. Enlarge 140% to return to original size.

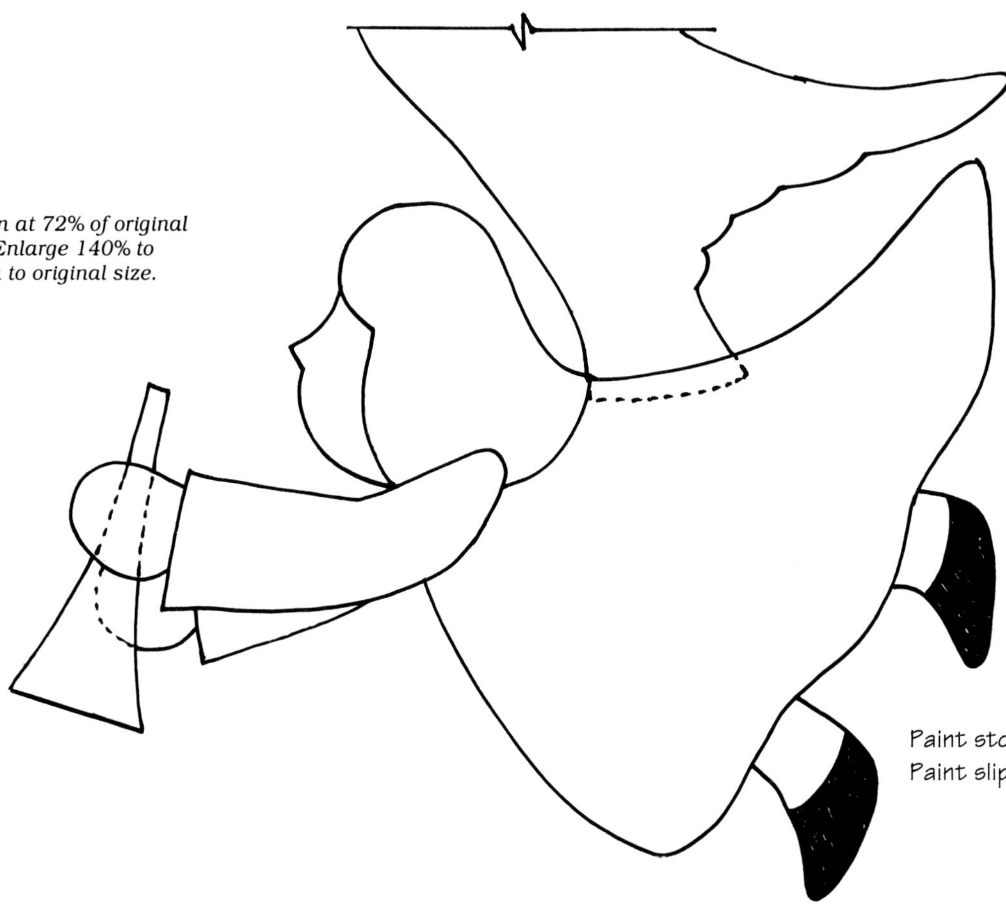

Paint stockings WHITE.
Paint slippers BLACK.

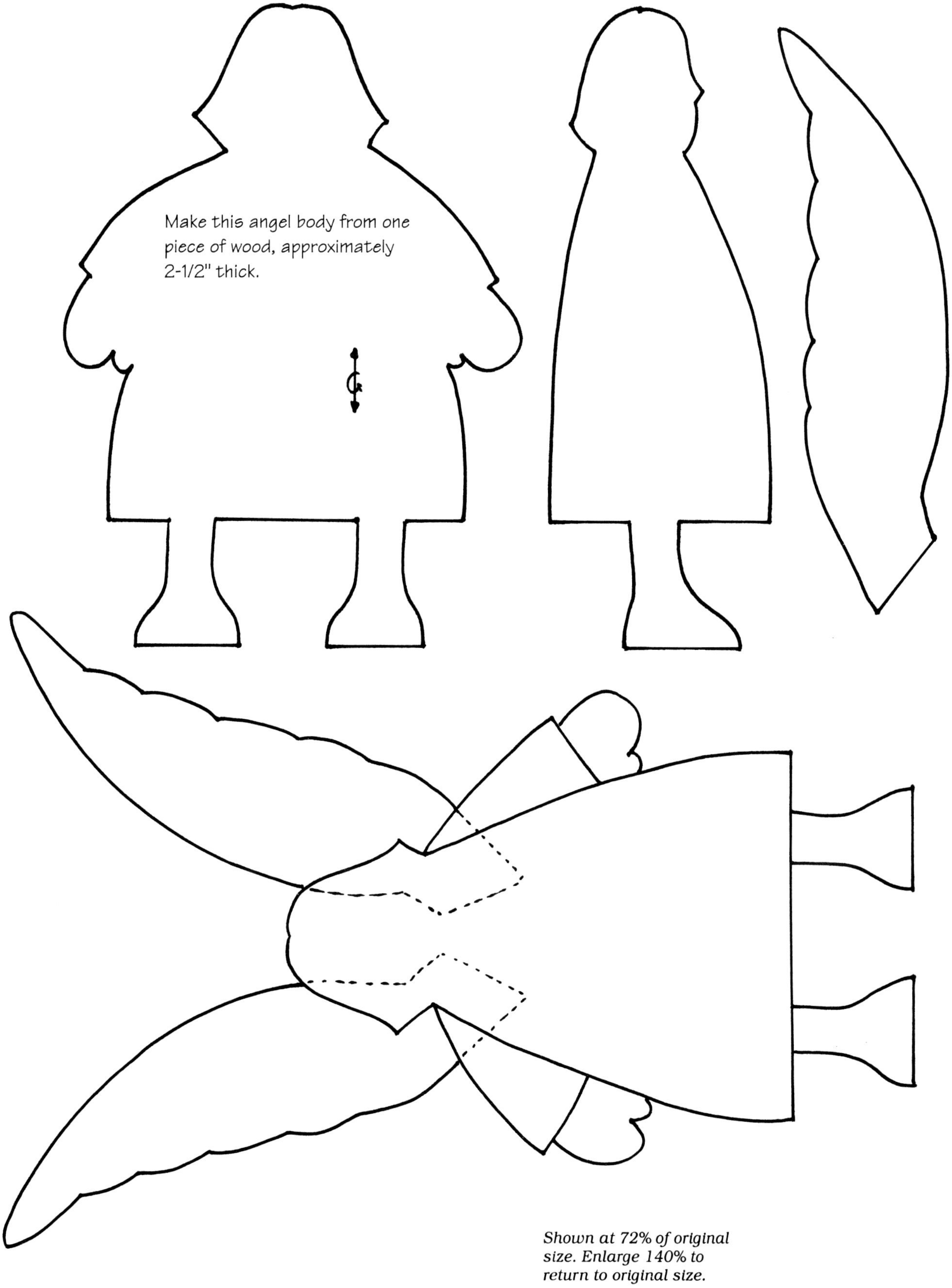

Shown at 72% of original size. Enlarge 140% to return to original size.

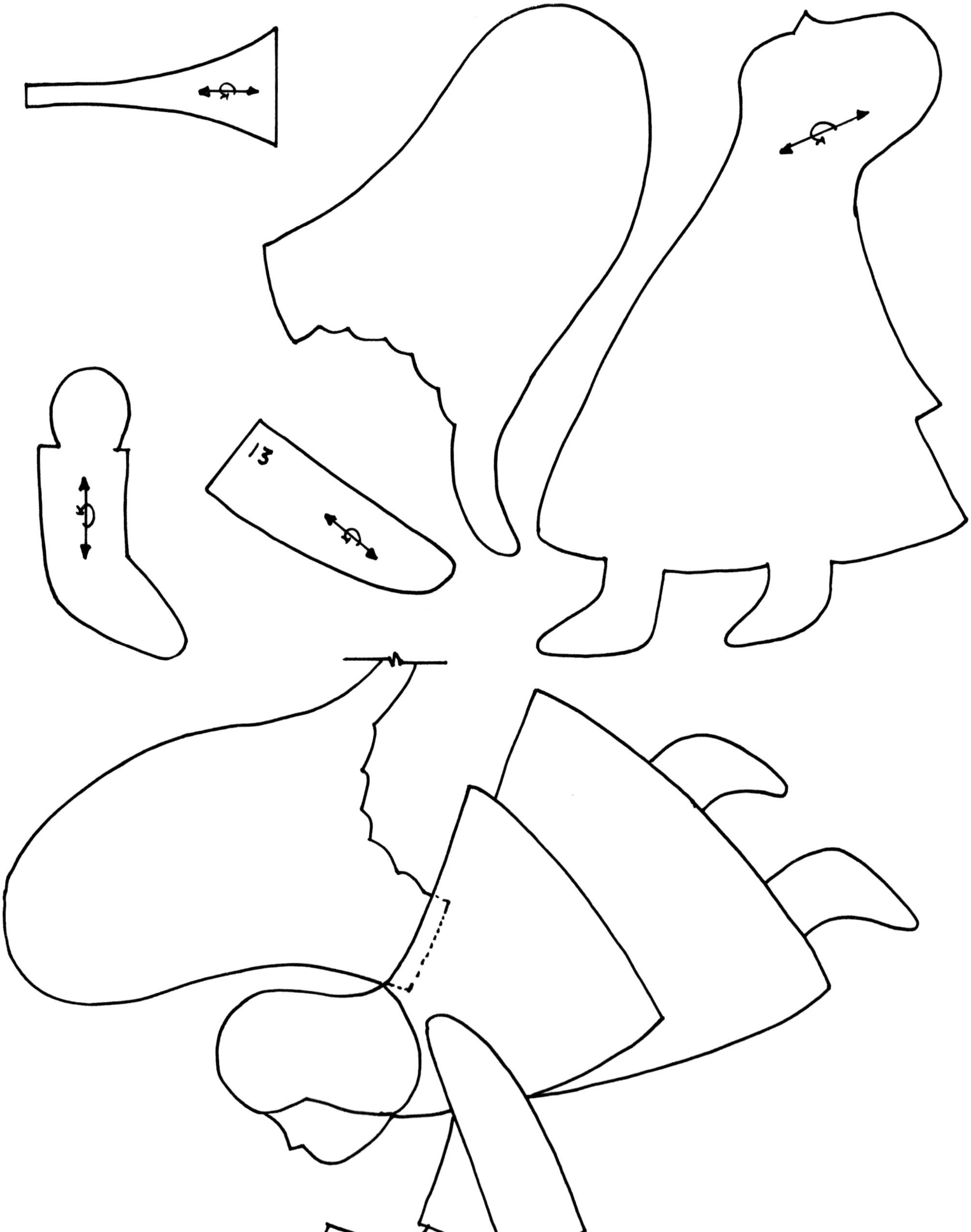

Shown at 72% of original size. Enlarge 140% to return to original size.

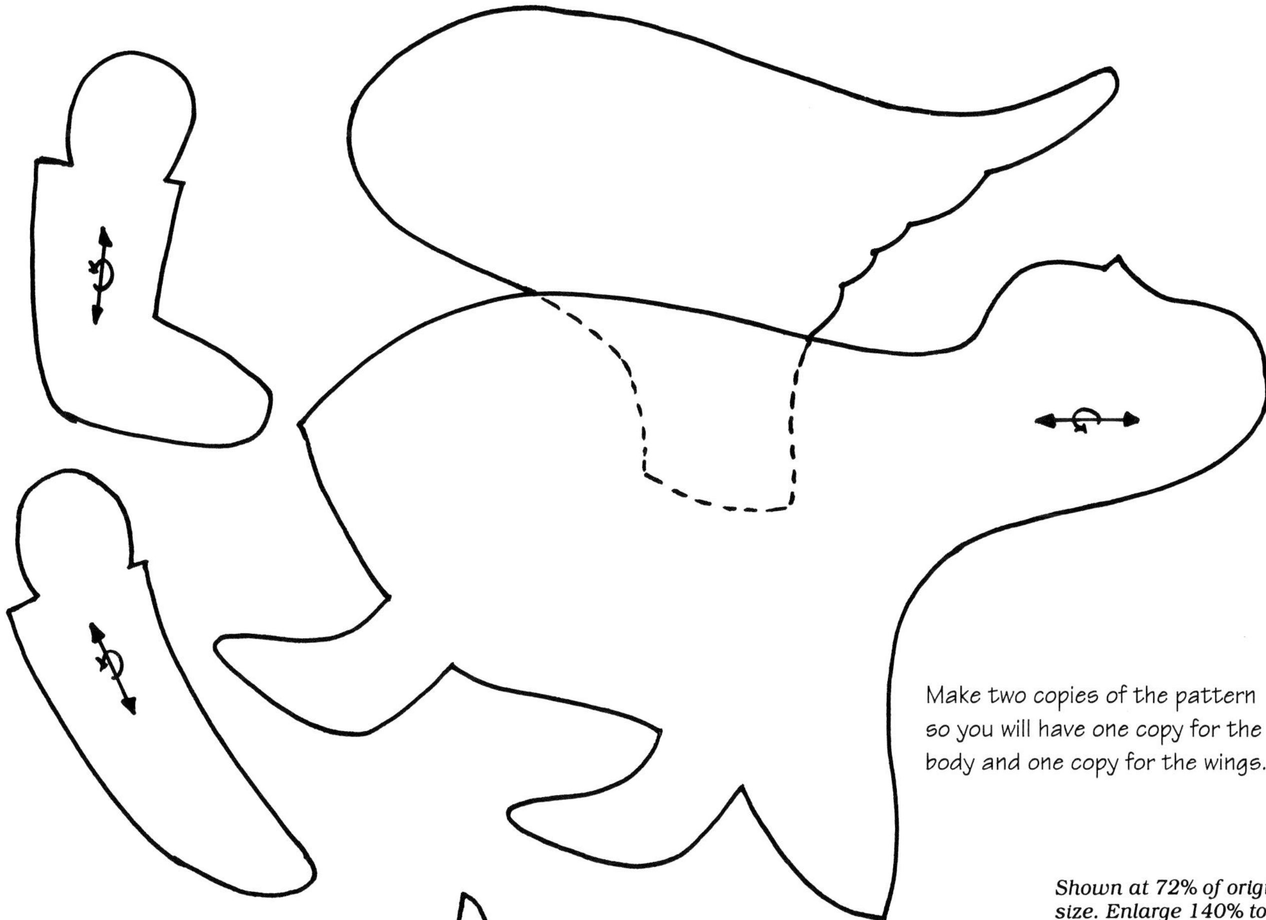

Make two copies of the pattern so you will have one copy for the body and one copy for the wings.

Shown at 72% of original size. Enlarge 140% to return to original size.

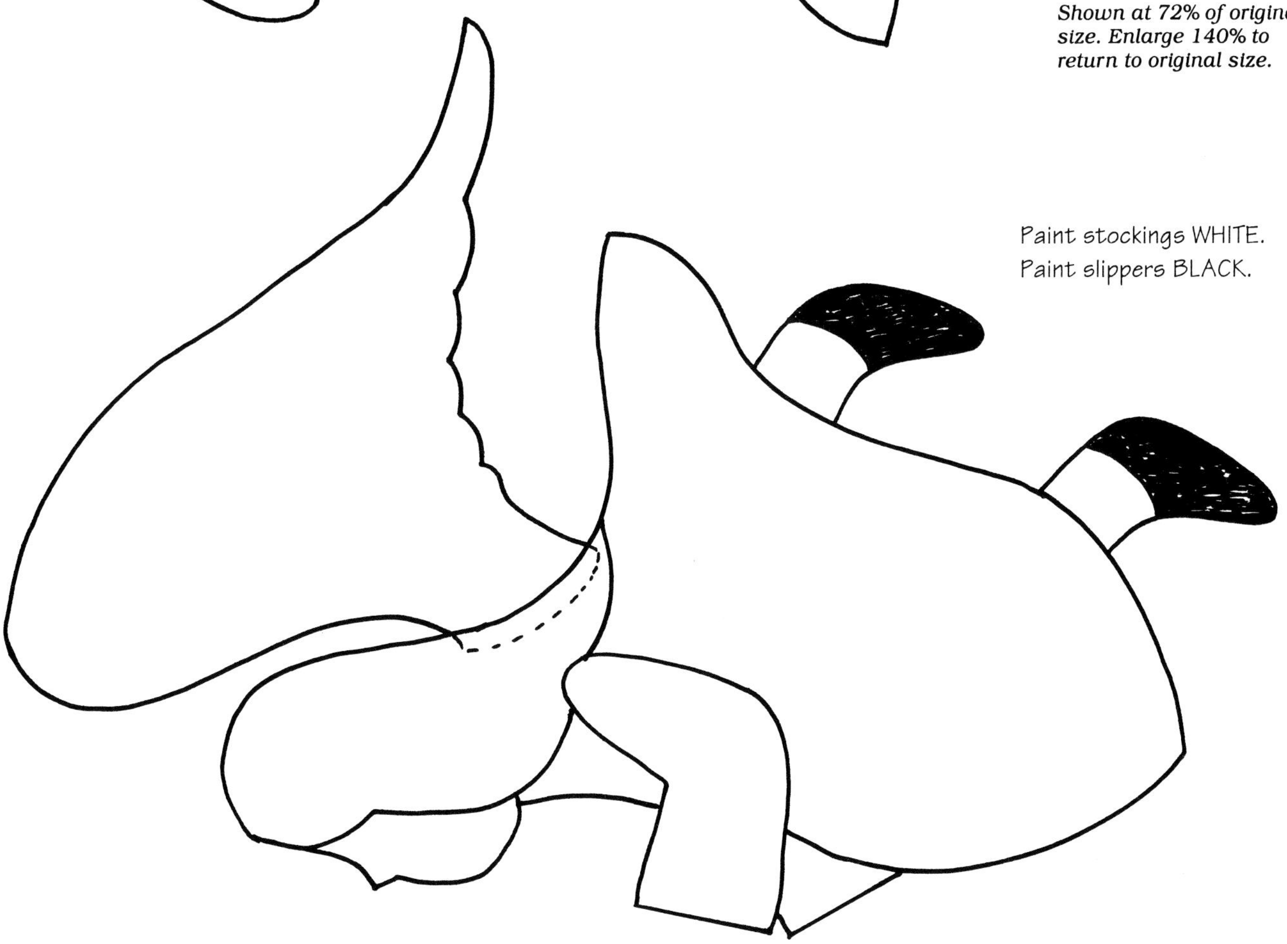

Paint stockings WHITE.
Paint slippers BLACK.

Use same pattern for both arms.

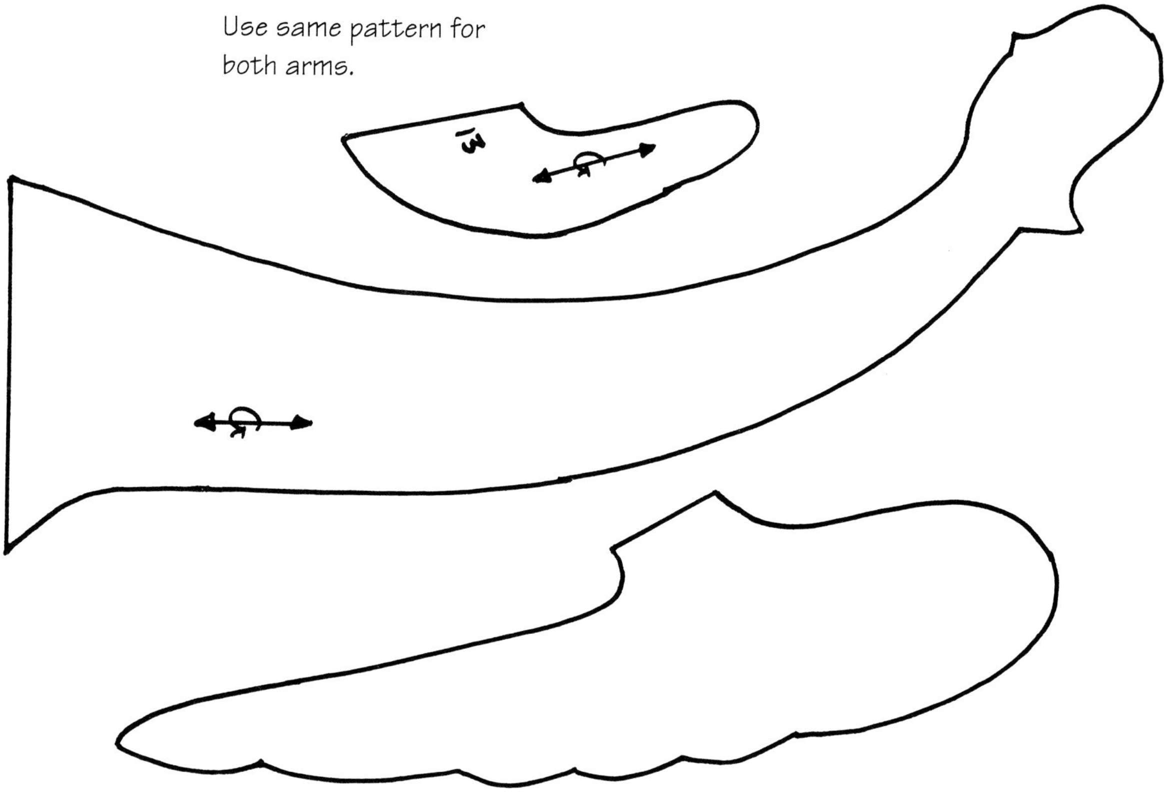

Shown at 72% of original size. Enlarge 140% to return to original size.

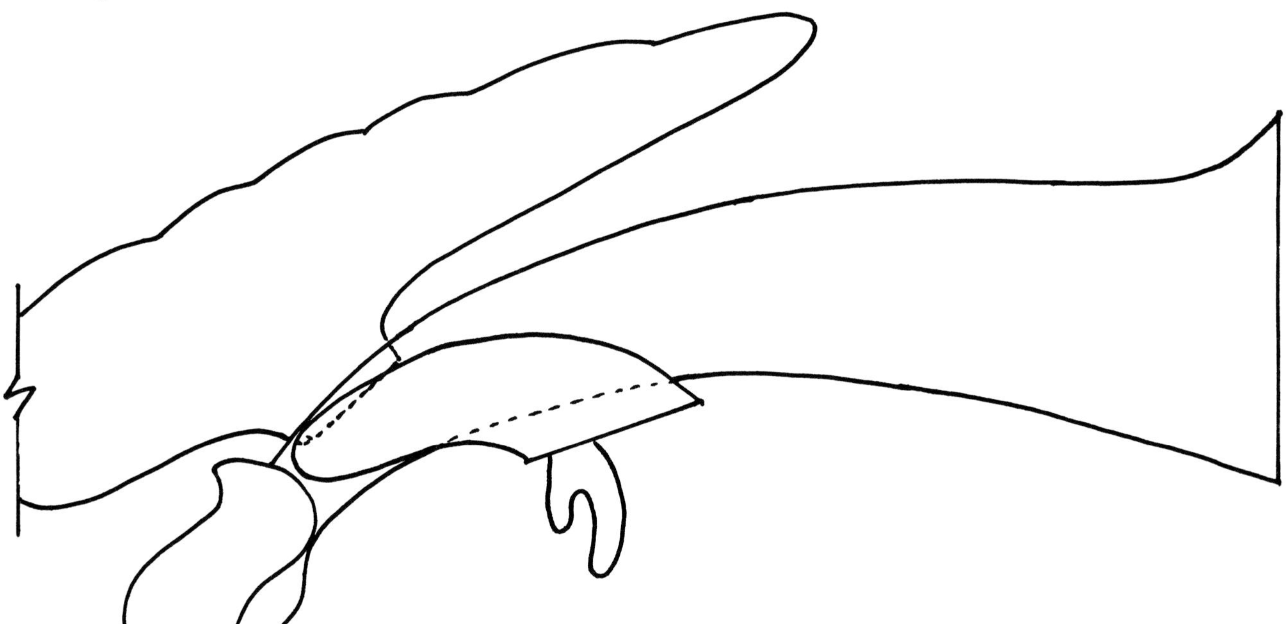

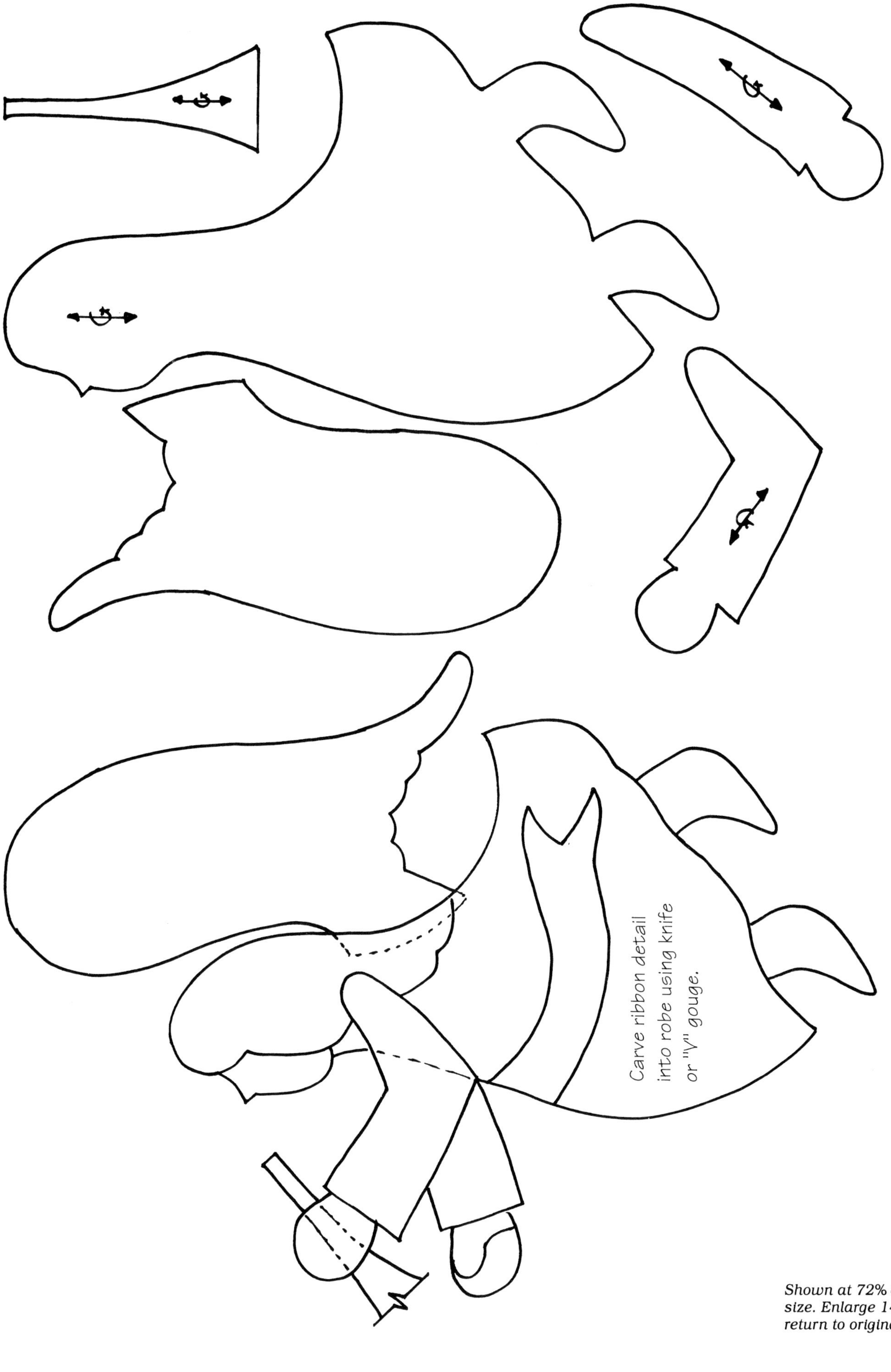

Shown at 72% of original size. Enlarge 140% to return to original size.

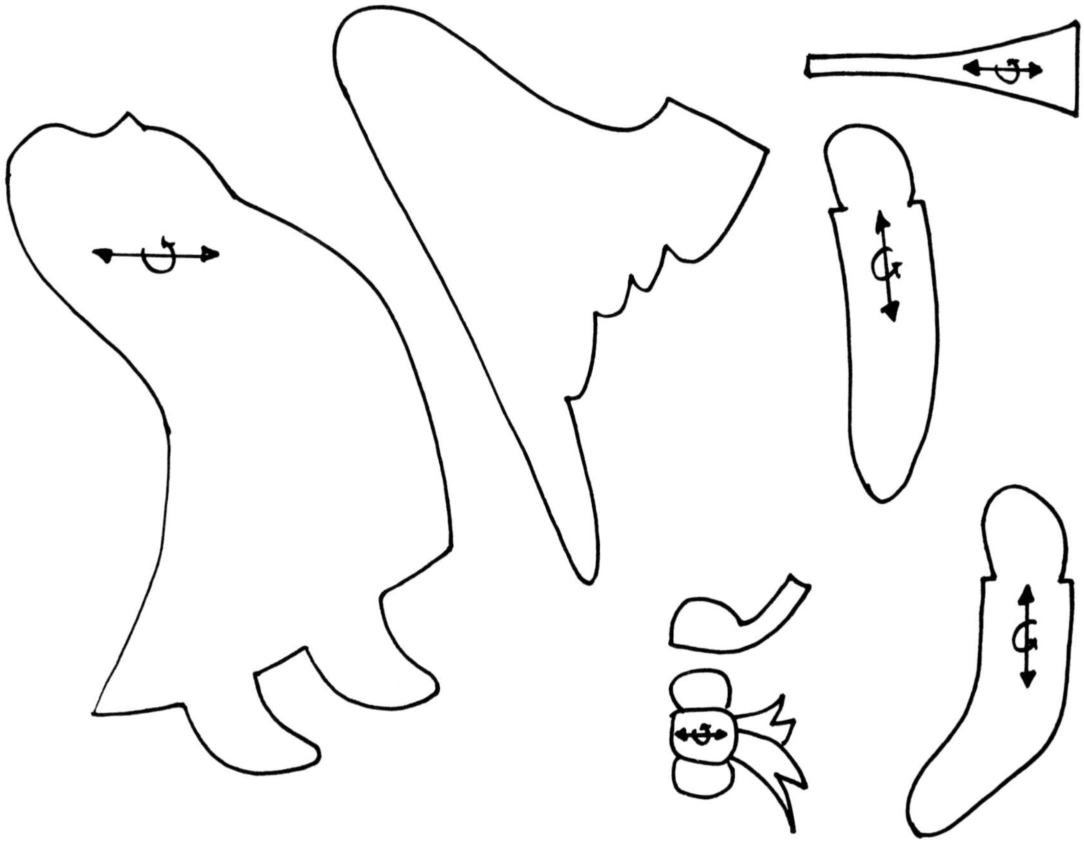

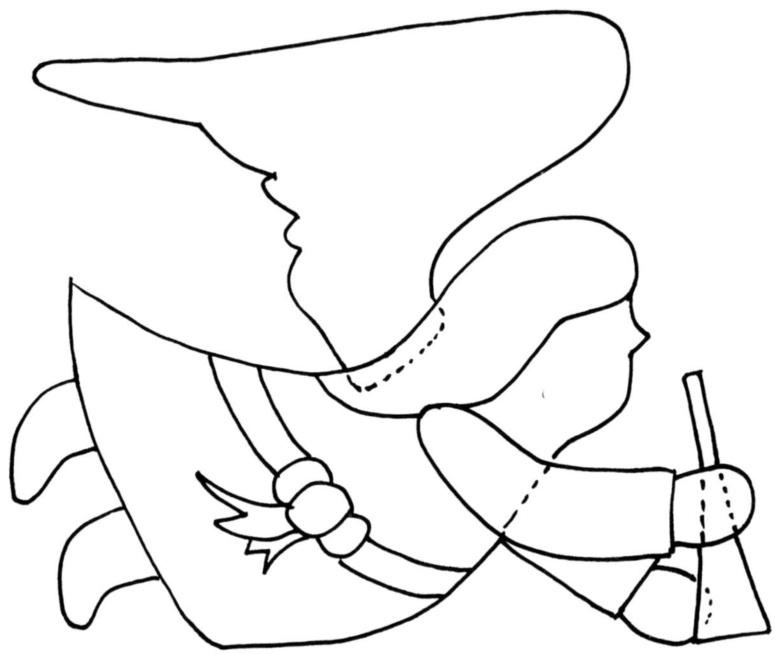

Shown at 72% of original size. Enlarge 140% to return to original size.

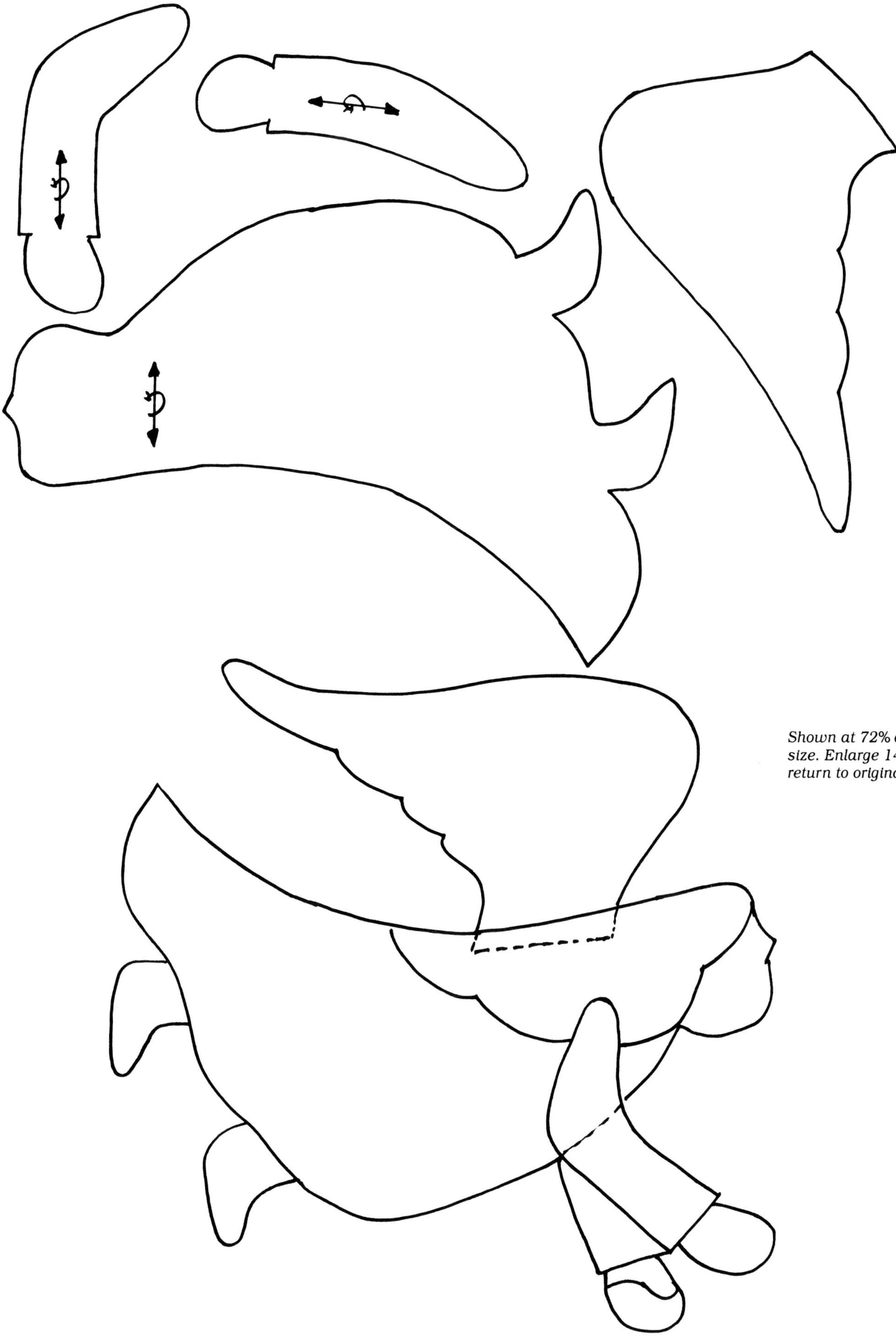

Shown at 72% of original size. Enlarge 140% to return to original size.

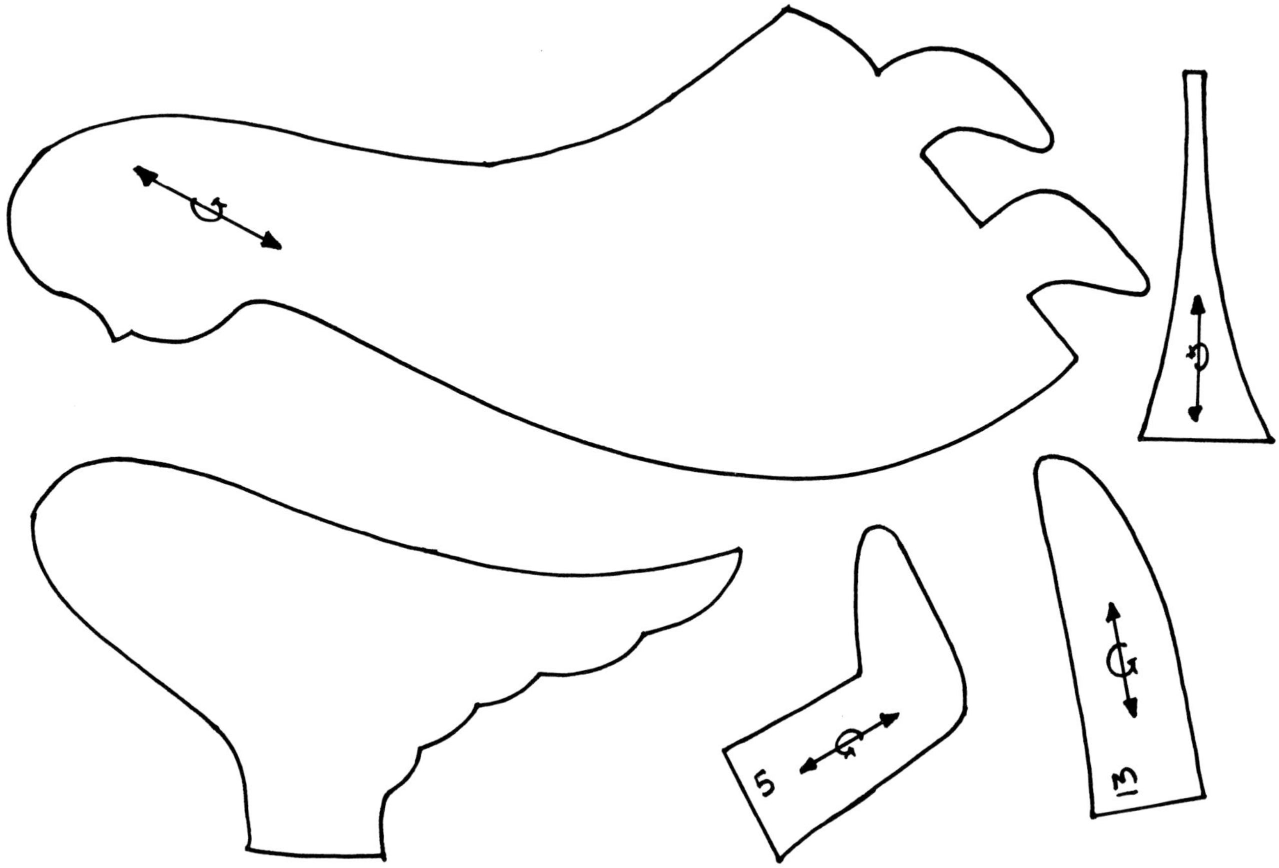

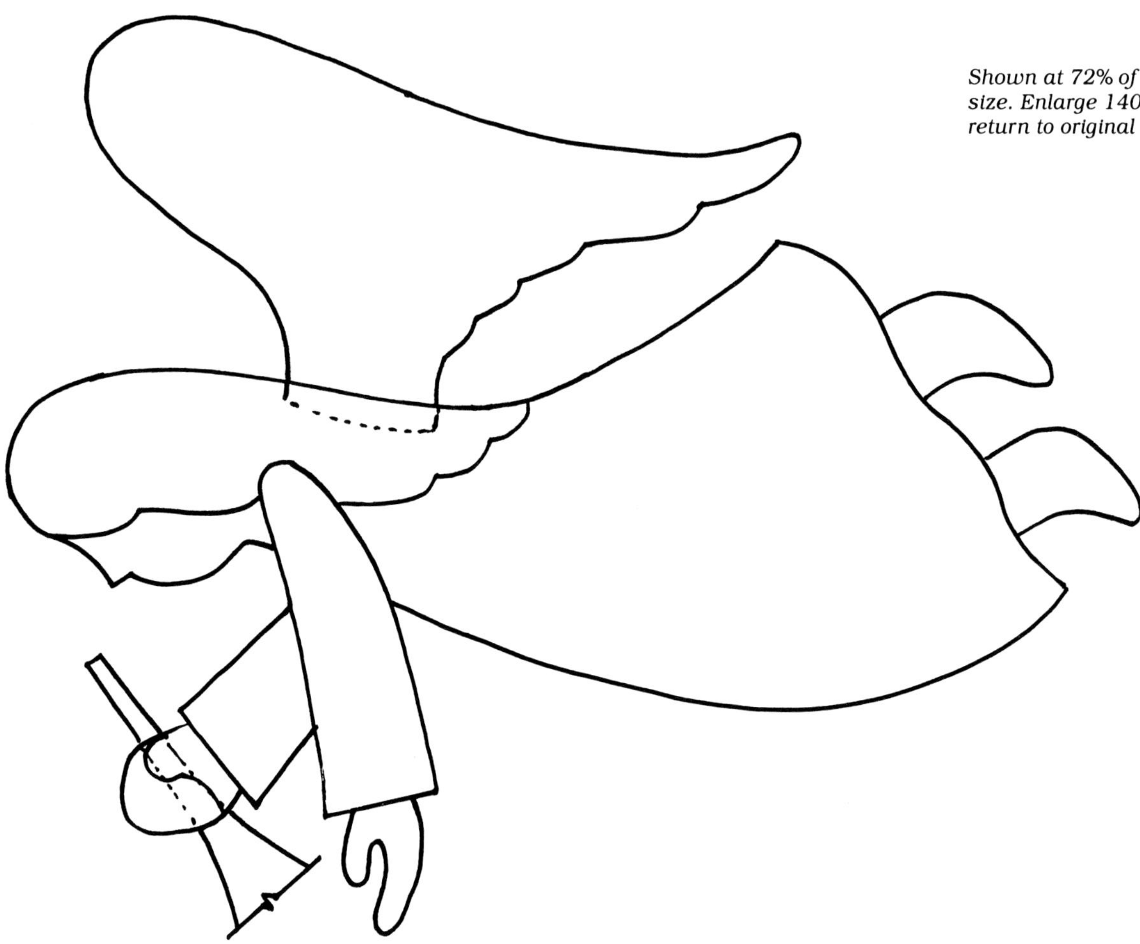

Shown at 72% of original size. Enlarge 140% to return to original size.

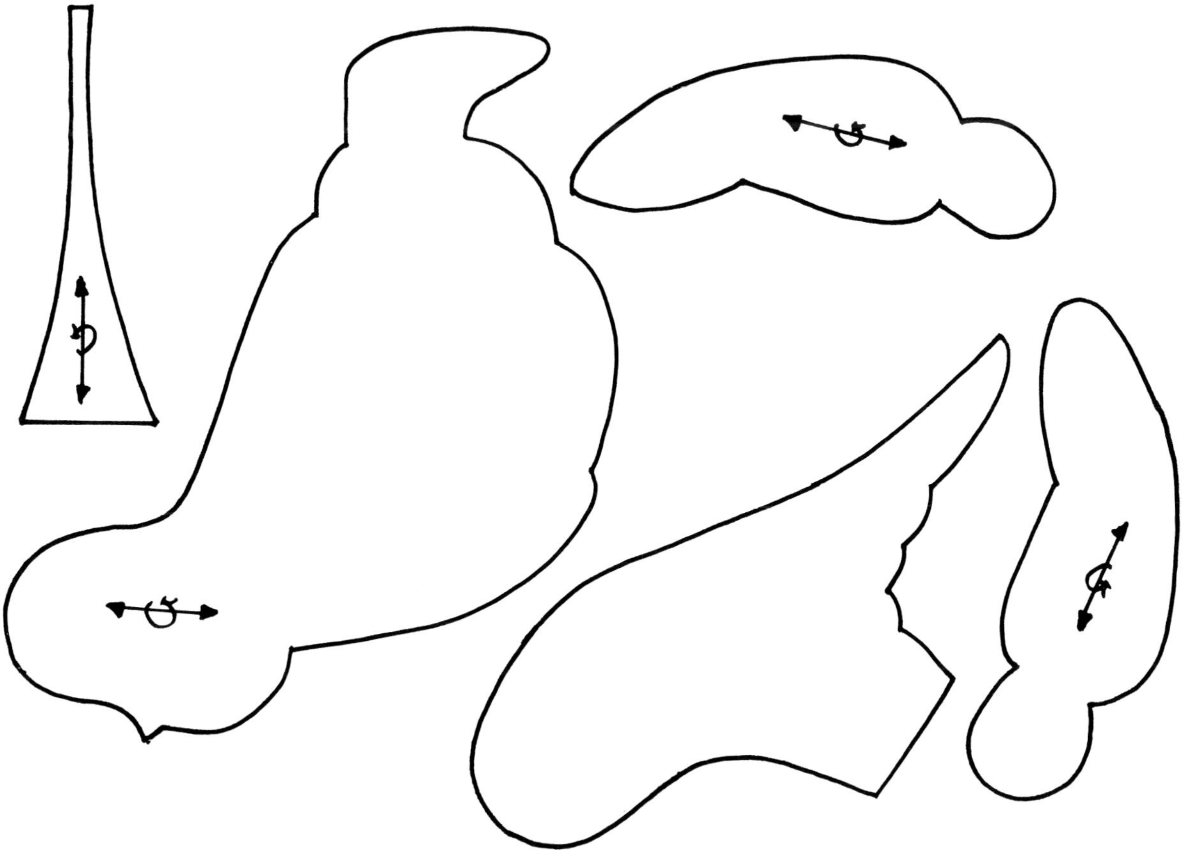

Shown at 72% of original size. Enlarge 140% to return to original size.

Paint Scheme:
Shirt.....BABY BLUE
Pants...MILK CHOCOLATE
Suspenders...LAMP BLACK
Suspender Buttons...VENETIAN GOLD

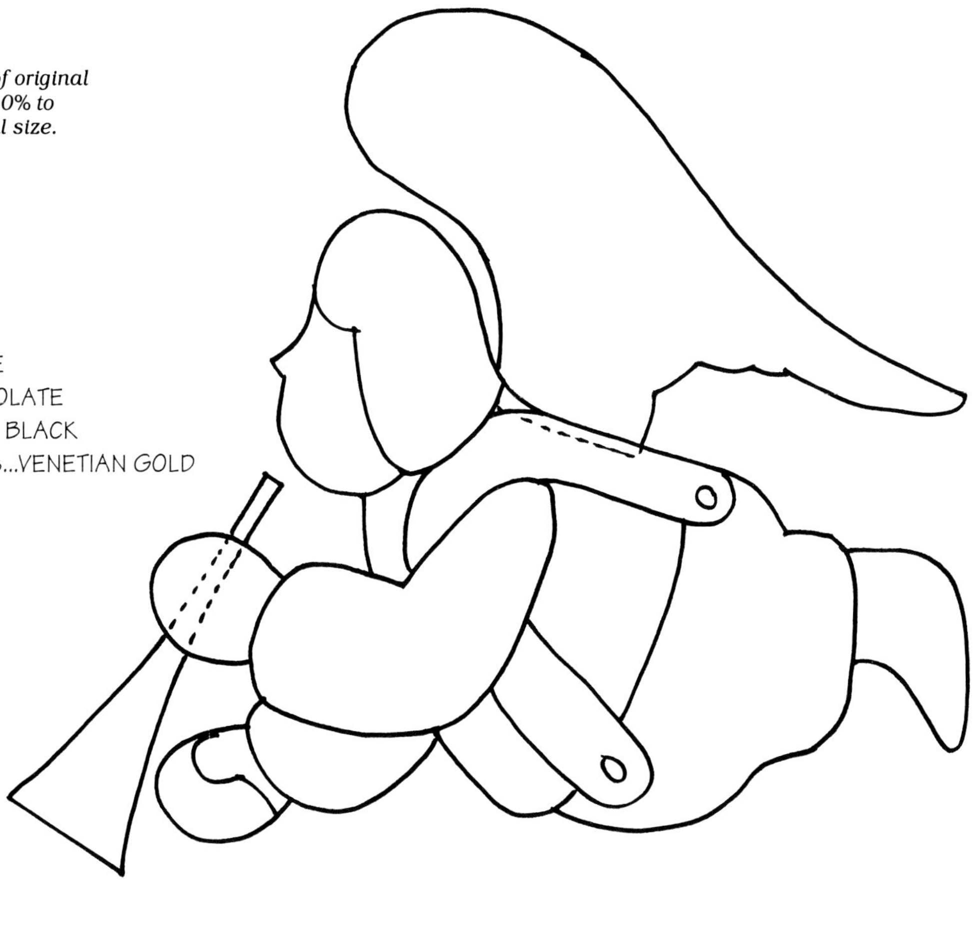

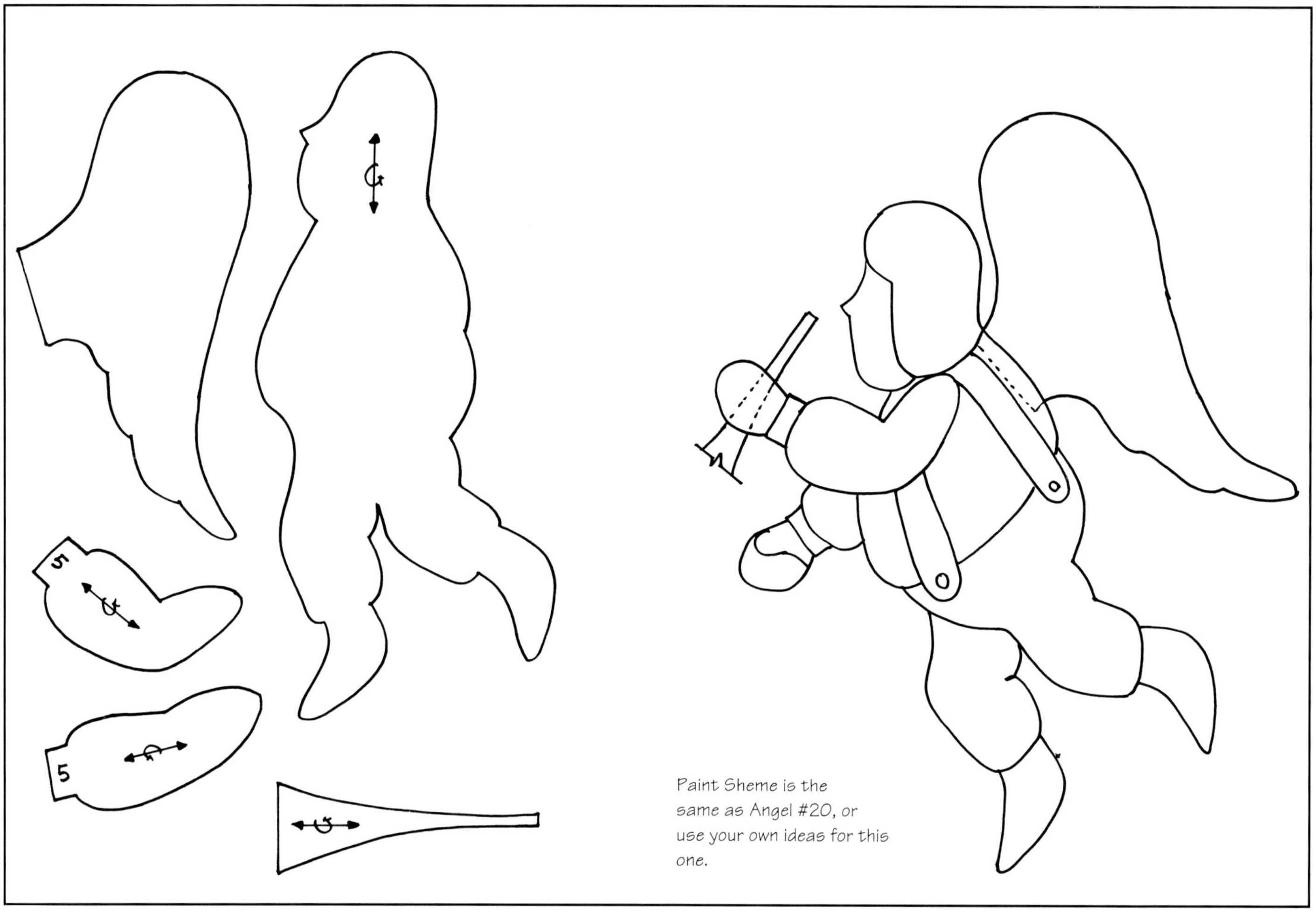

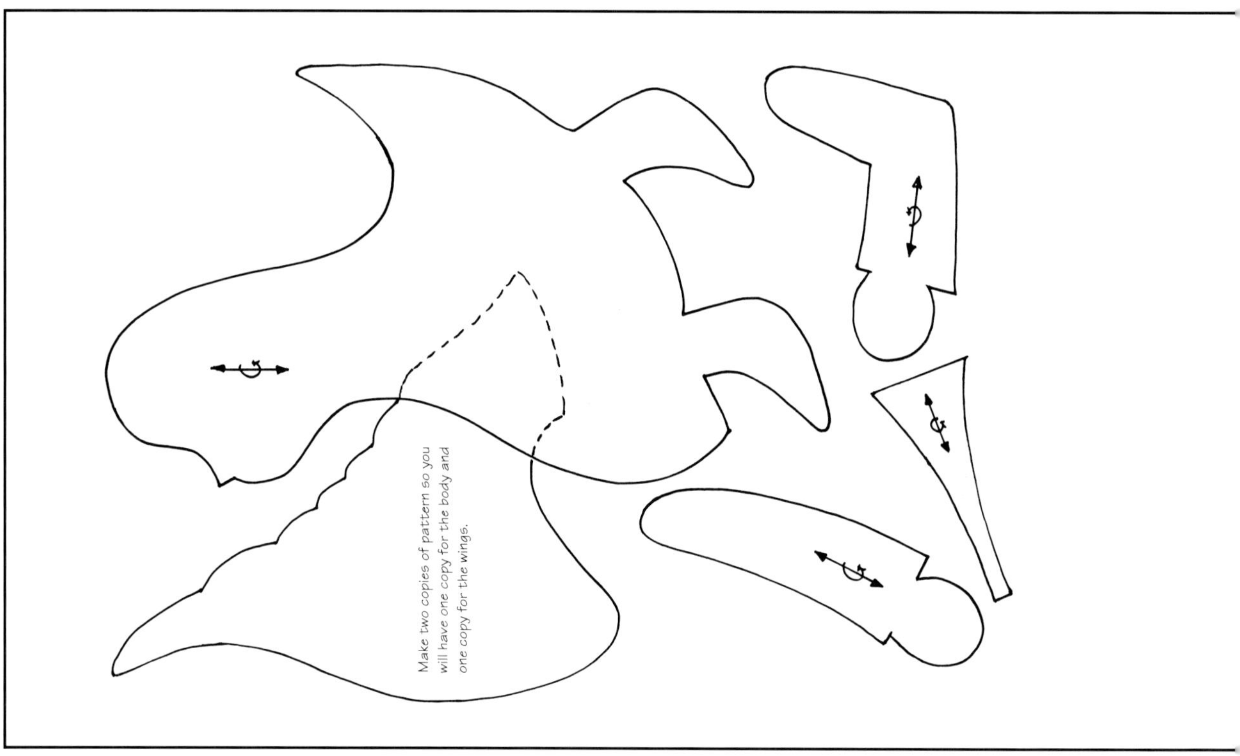

Shown at 50% of original size. Enlarge 200% to return to original size.

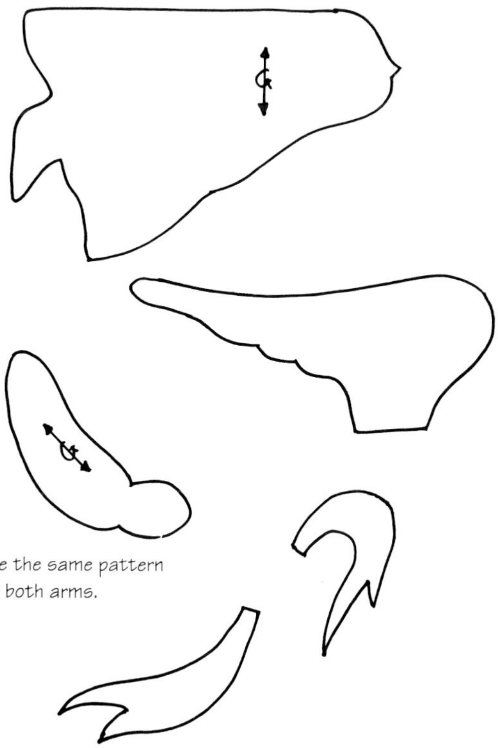

Jse the same pattern
'or both arms.

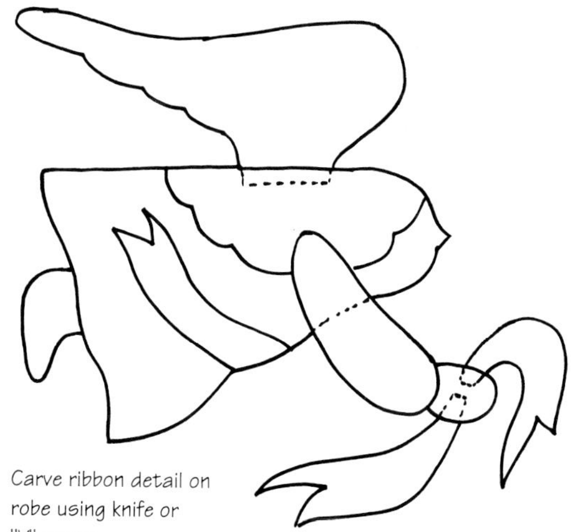

Carve ribbon detail on
robe using knife or
"V" gouge.

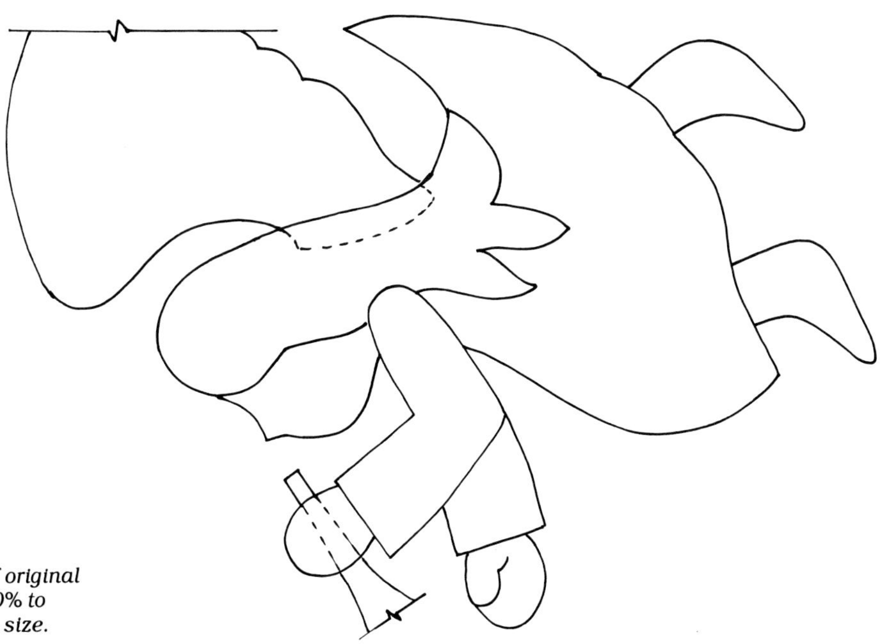

Shown at 50% of original size. Enlarge 200% to return to original size.

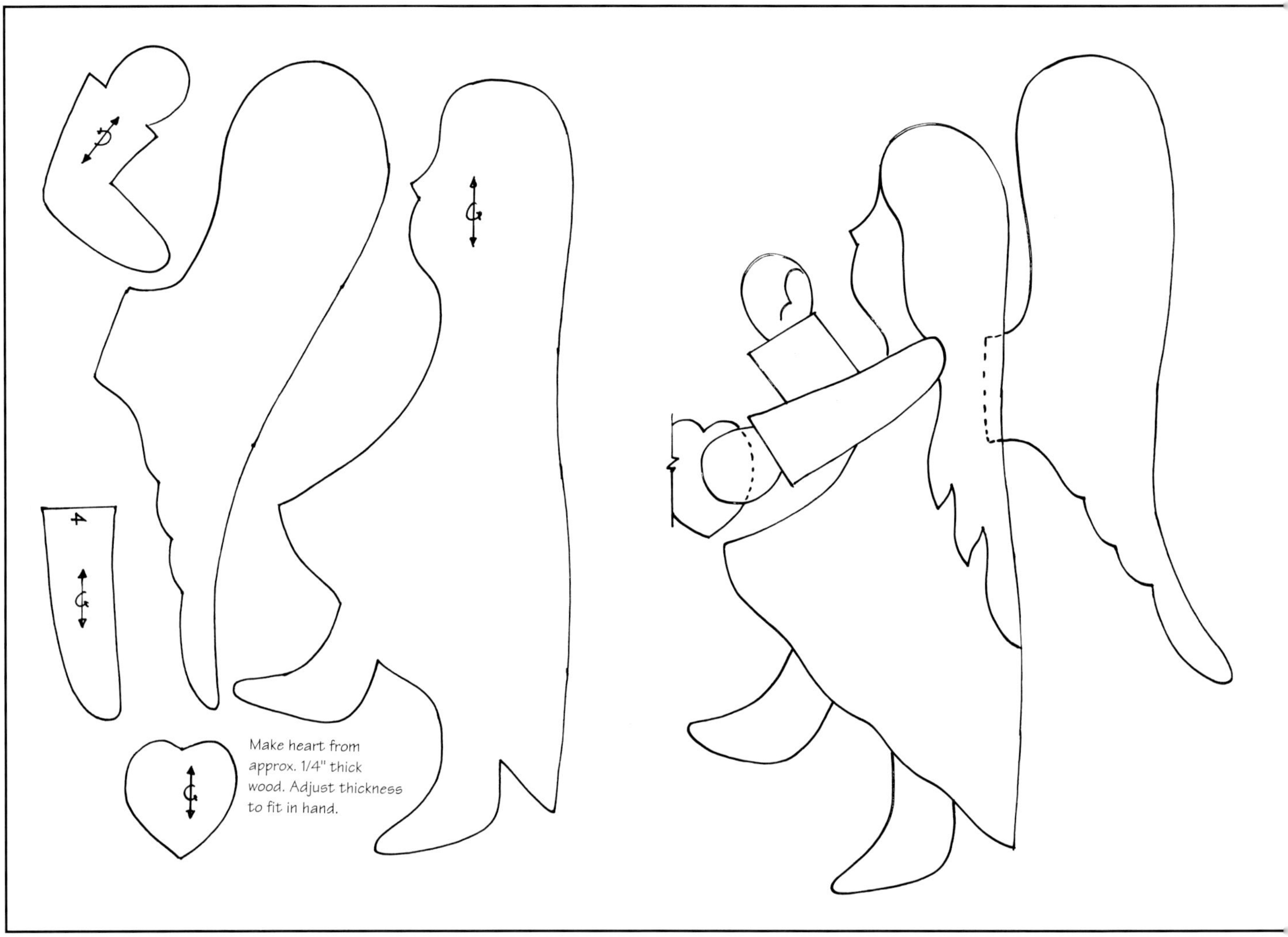

Shown at 50% of original size. Enlarge 200% to return to original size.

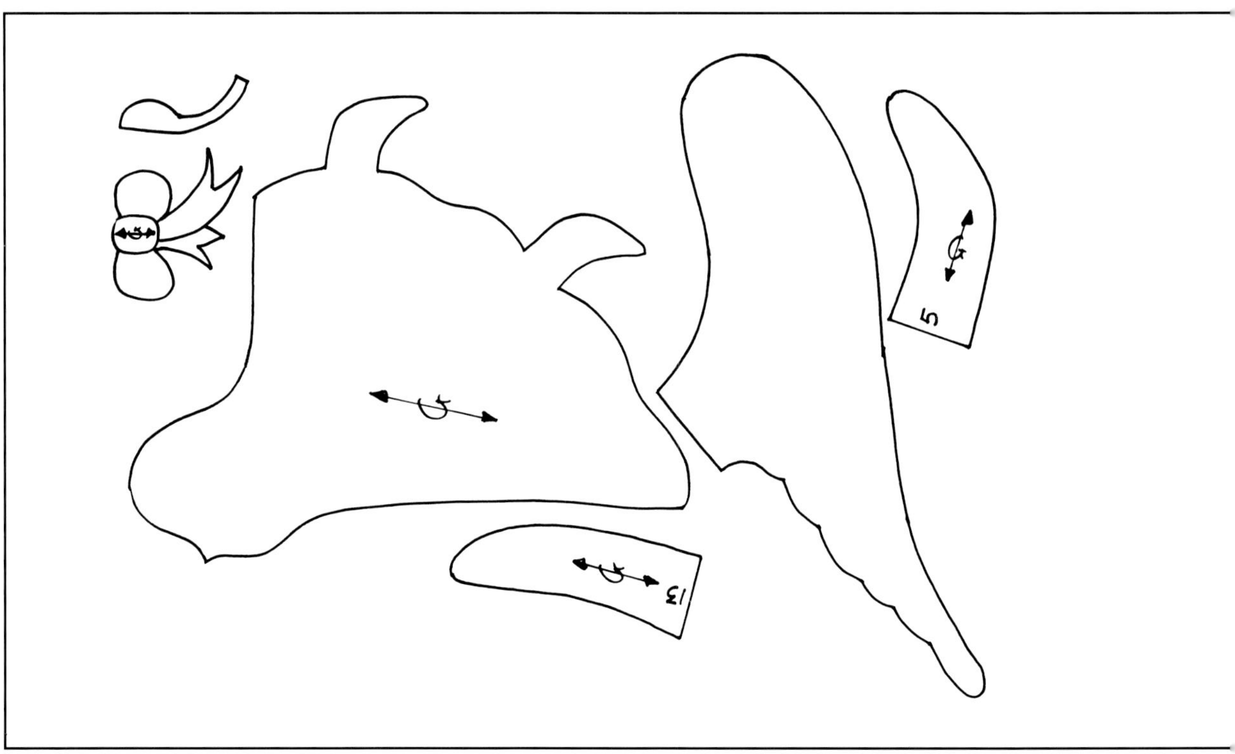

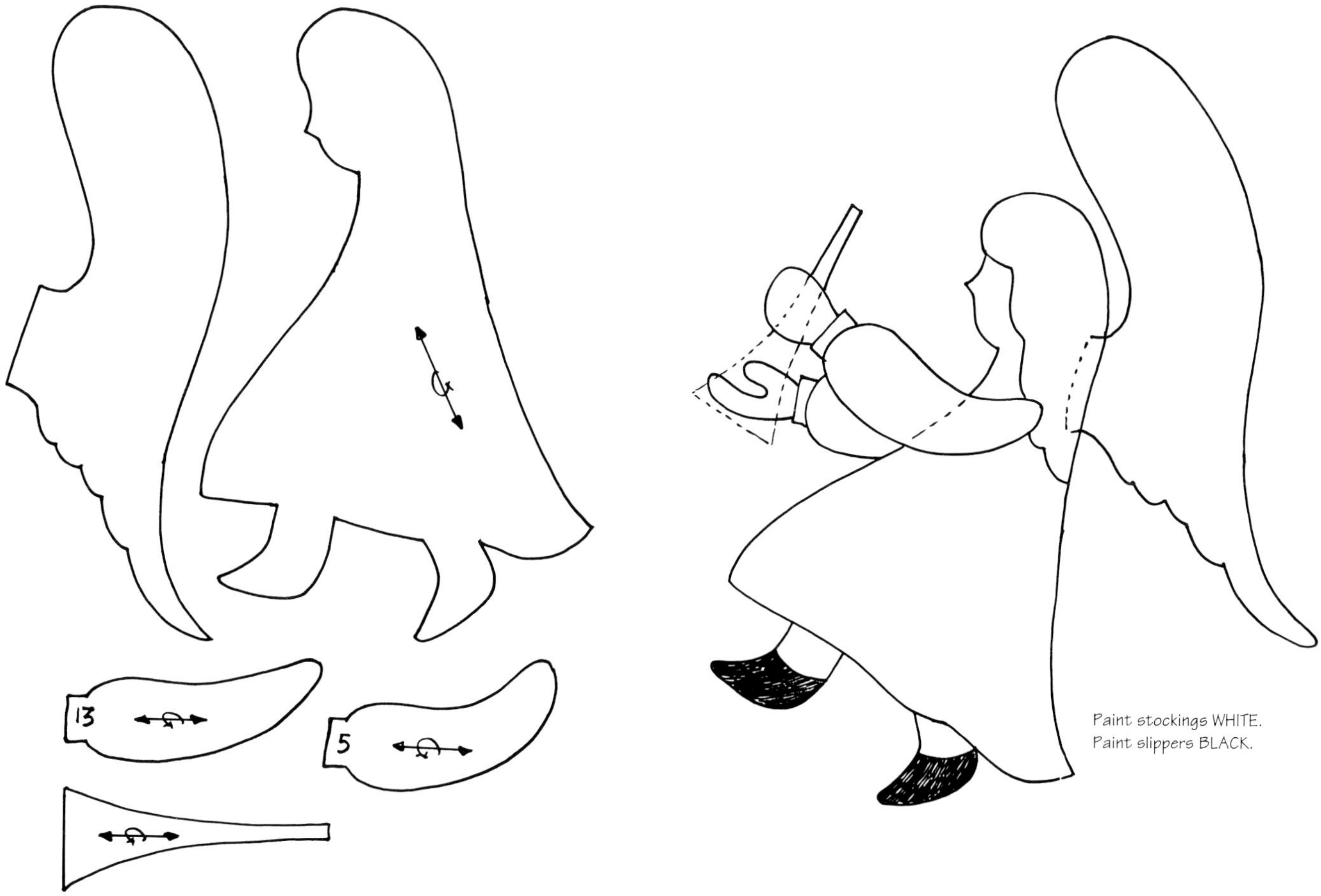

Shown at 50% of original size. Enlarge 200% to return to original size.

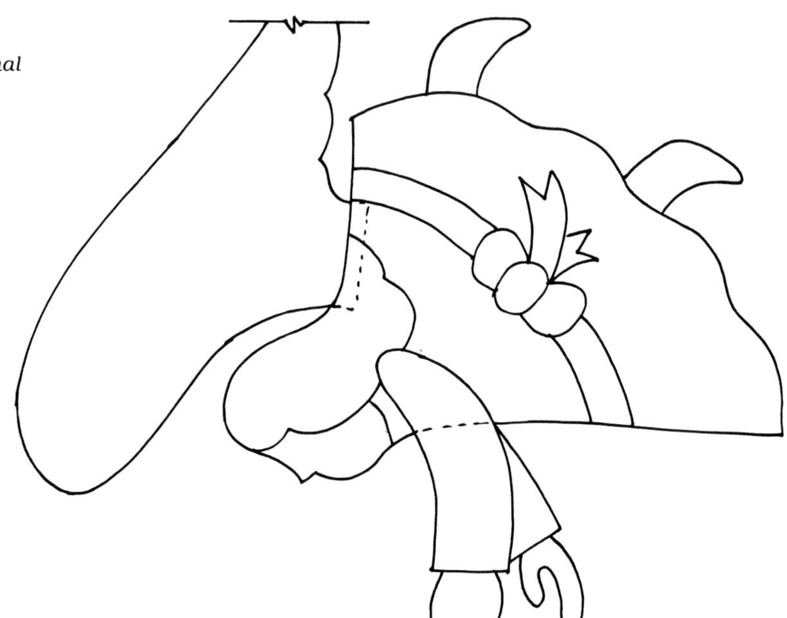

THE PROJECT PATTERN

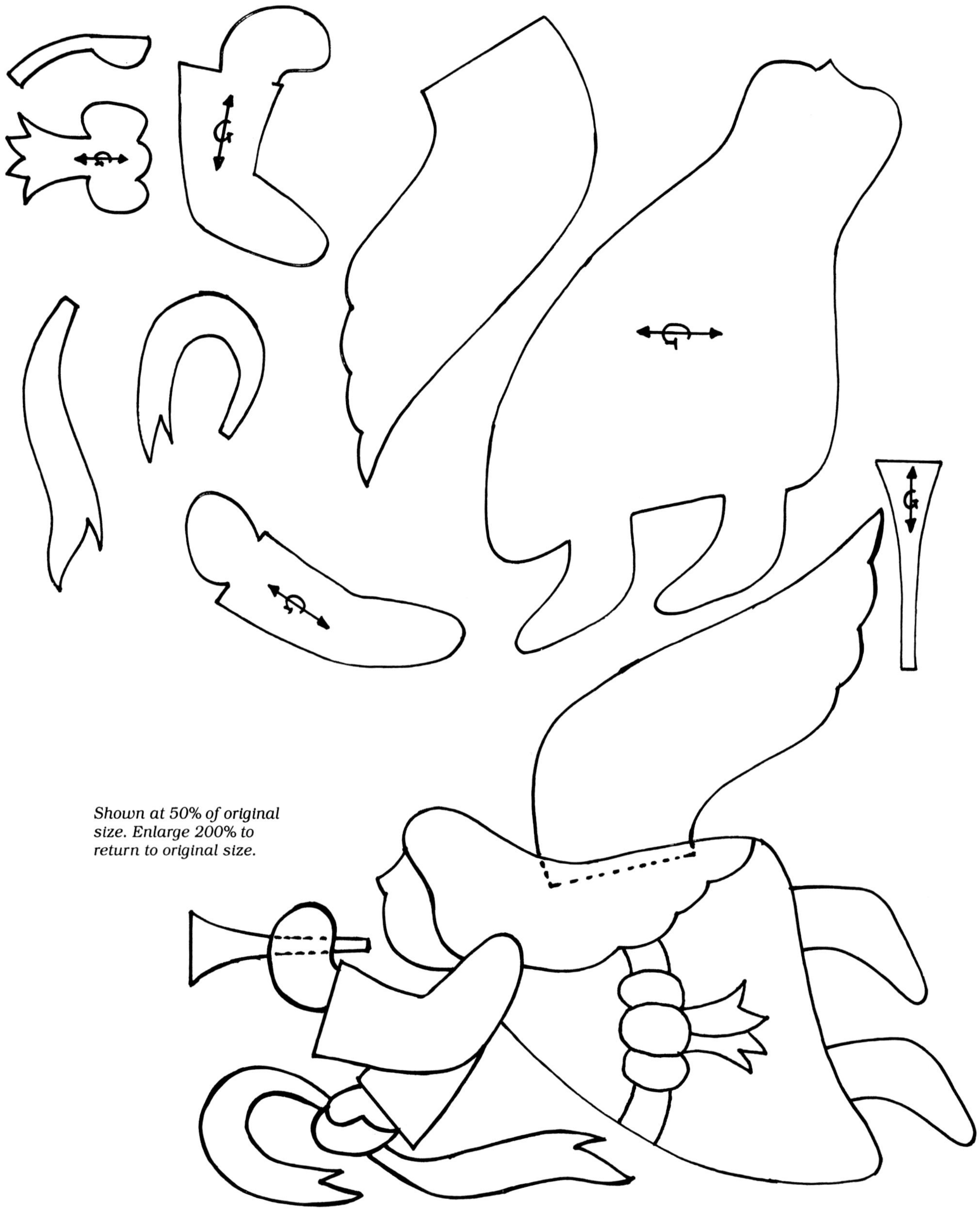

Shown at 50% of original size. Enlarge 200% to return to original size.

CARVING THE PROJECT

Carving the Body

Transfer the pattern outlines to the proper thicknesses of wood, as suggested in the Introduction of this book. I will be using 1-3/4" thick Basswood for the body of this angel. After transferring the patterns to the wood, saw out the pieces using a bandsaw if possible. *DO NOT saw out the horn or bow yet.* I will discuss them later in the carving sequence.

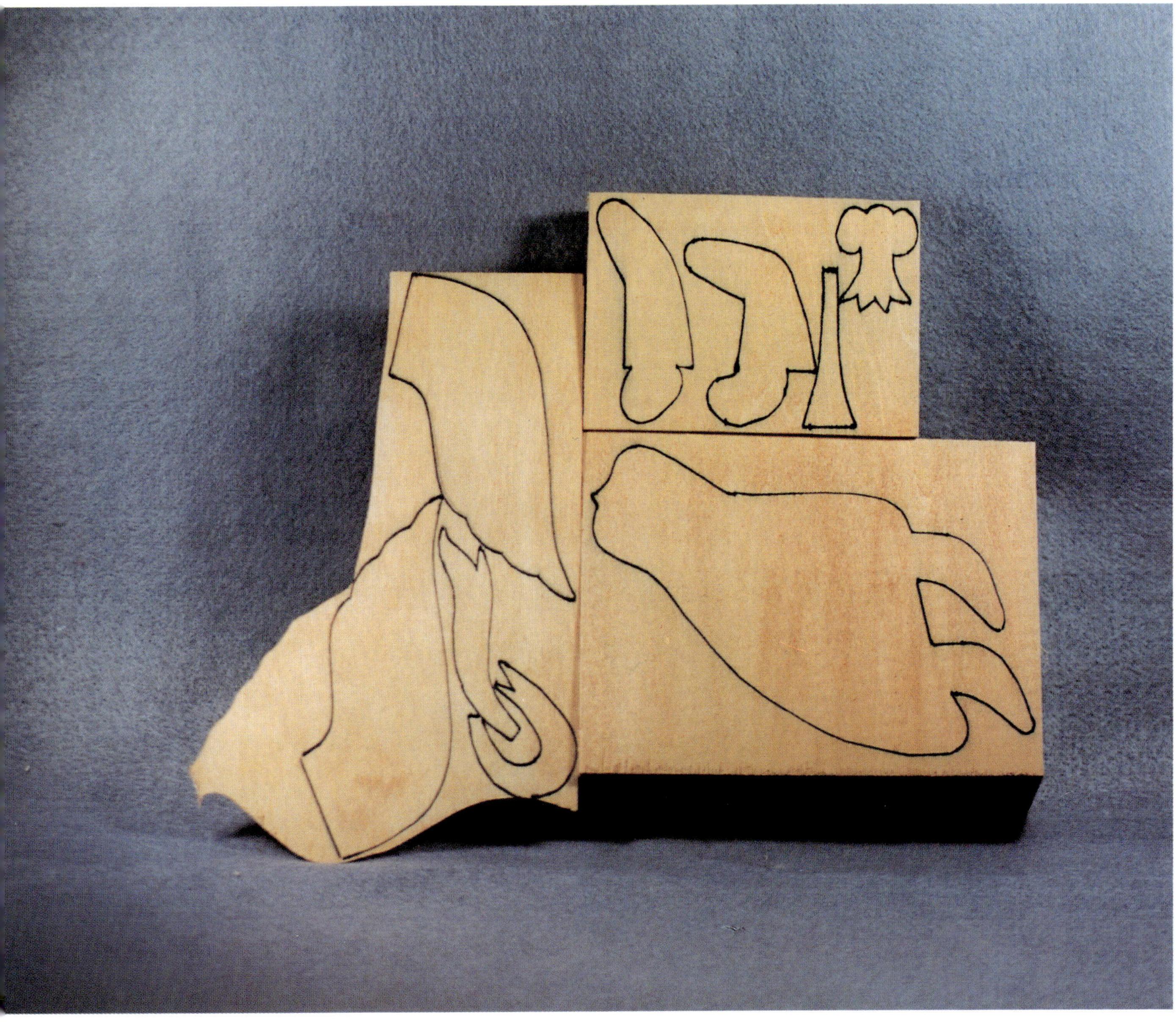

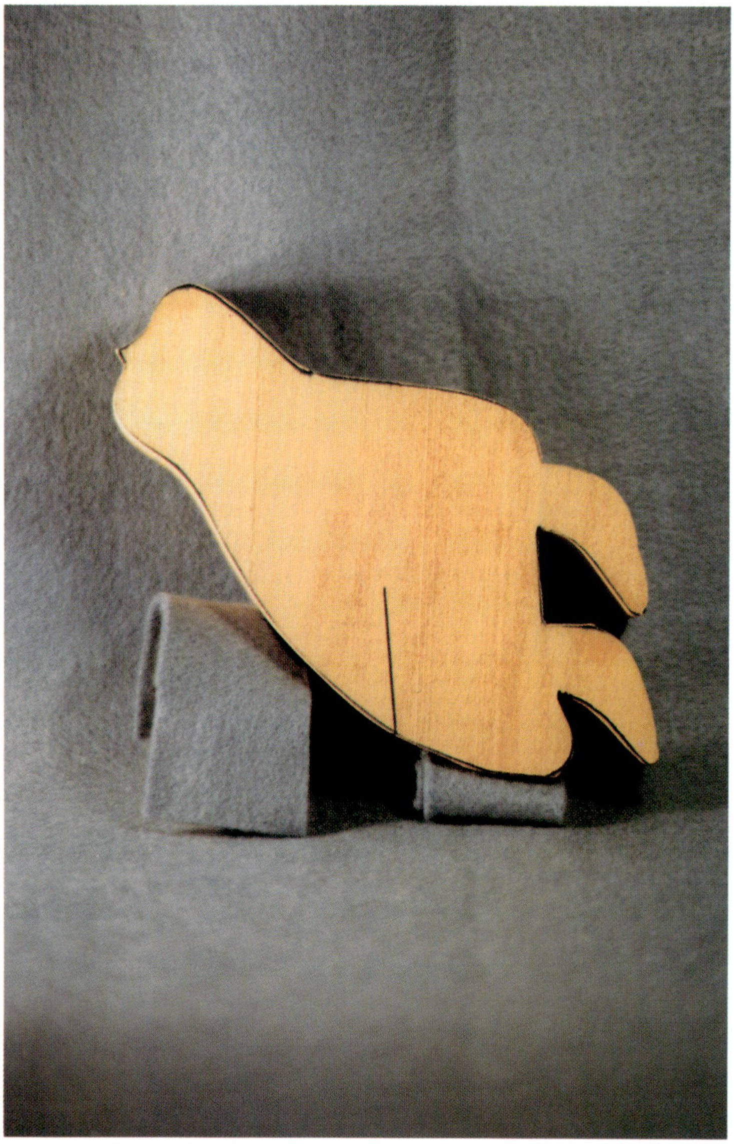

Choose the angle that you want your angel to assume when mounted on its base, and sketch a line down one side of the body as a reference.

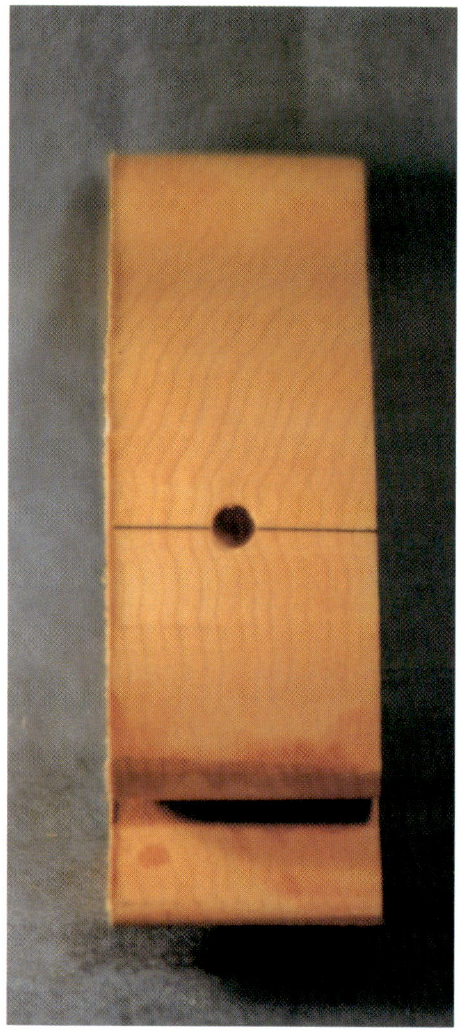

Continue this line around to the underside, and mark the center of the body. Using a drill or drill press with a 5/16" bit, drill into the body approximately 3/4" deep, using the line you sketched on the side of the body as your reference angle.

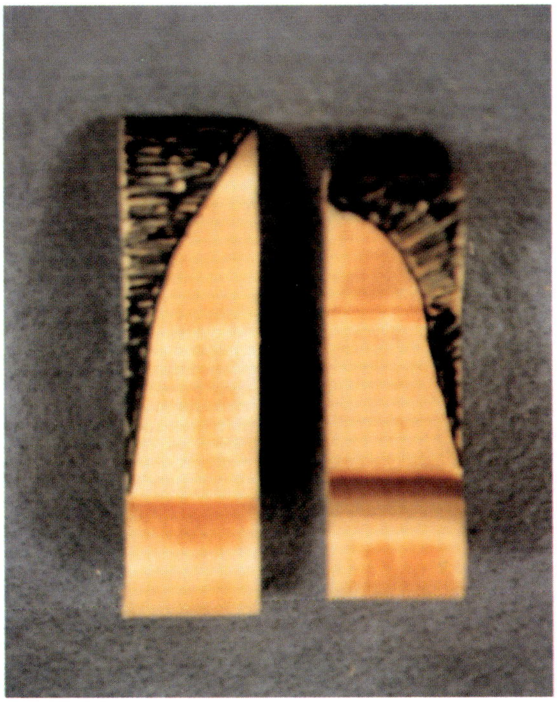

Now that you have the arms sawn out, lay them on their edge and sketch in a taper from the end of the sleeve up to the shoulder joint (as represented by the darkened area on the arms in the photo).

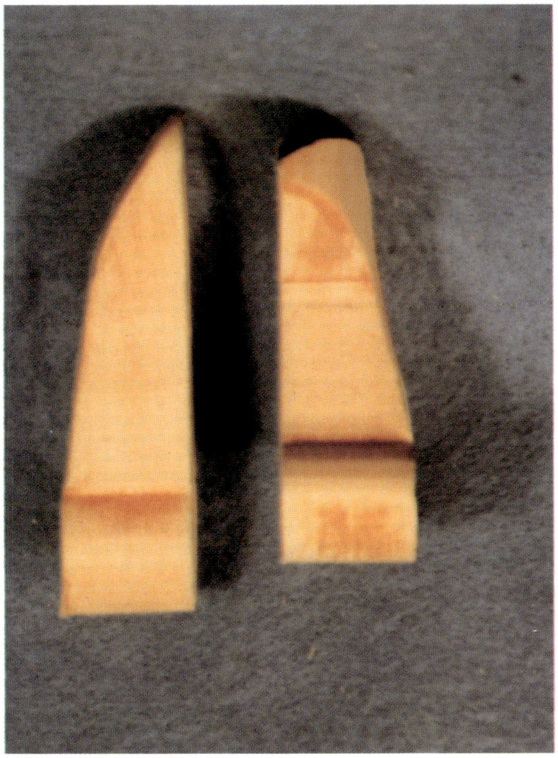

Using caution, saw this darkened area away from both arms.

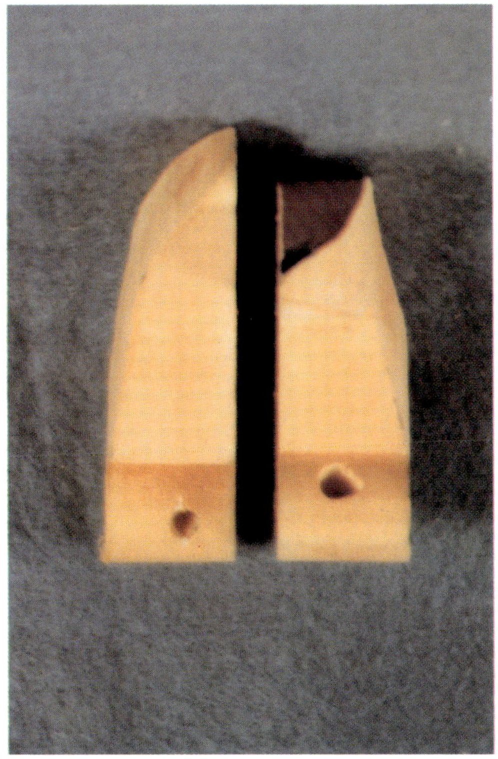

Now, since our angel is going to be holding some objects, we need holes in her hands. Using a drill with a 3/16" bit in it, drill down and go completely through both hands. Leave a little extra wood toward the front of the hands in order to make the next step easier. (The pattern shows a suggested angle for the holes through the hands).

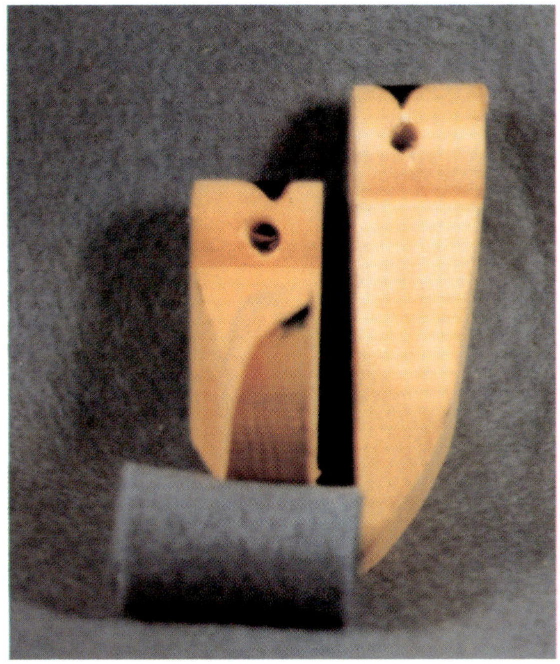

Sketch the top view of the hands (thumb and closed fingers) as shown in the photo by the darkened wood.

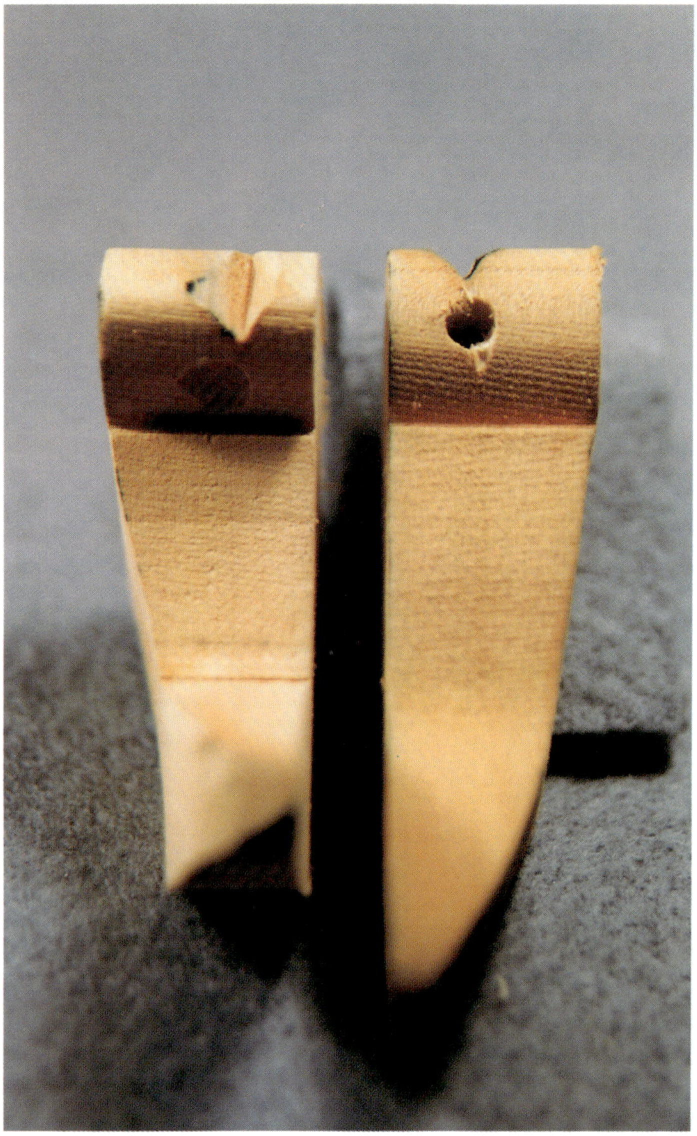

Again, using caution, saw away this darkened area from both hands. We now have two arms and hands that will require very little work to complete, later in the carving sequence.

At this point, before any carving on the body is started, you need to establish the arm positions on the body. Hold the left arm flat against the body as suggested by the pattern, or at a different angle if you desire (here is where you have a lot of flexibility in the poses), and trace the outline of the arm onto the body. Repeat this process for the right arm.

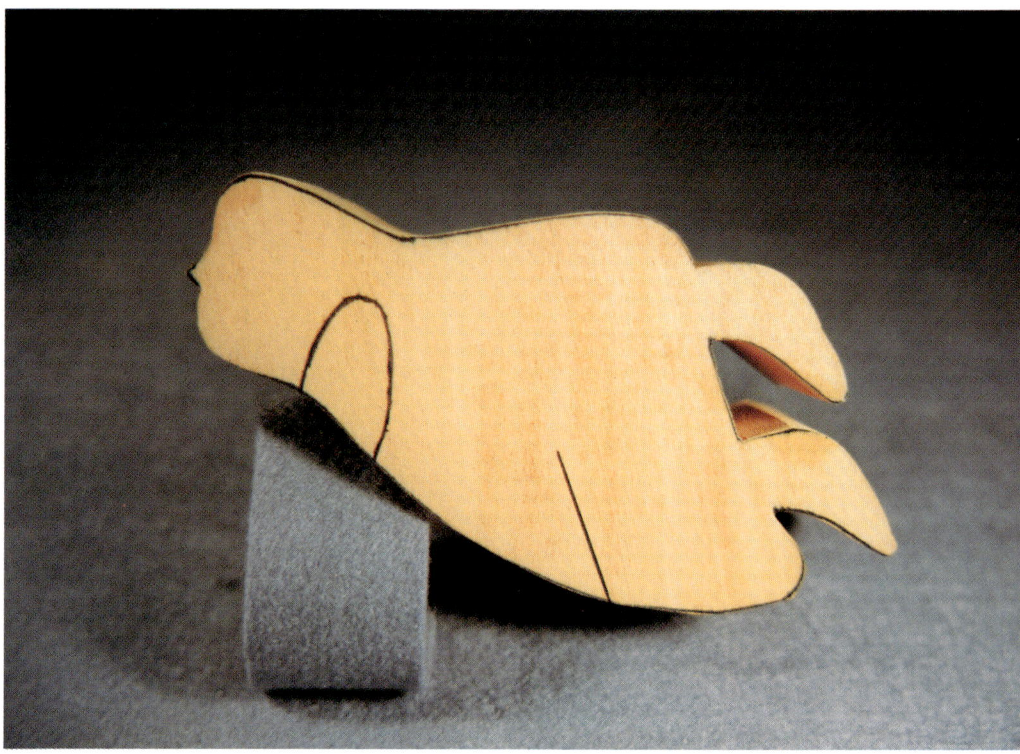

You have now established some of my famous **"NO-CARVE"** zones, as indicated by the darkened area in the photo. The side areas of these zones must be kept flat during the carving process so the arms will fit flush to the body when we assemble the angel later. Now, put the arms away for a while, and let's get started on the body.

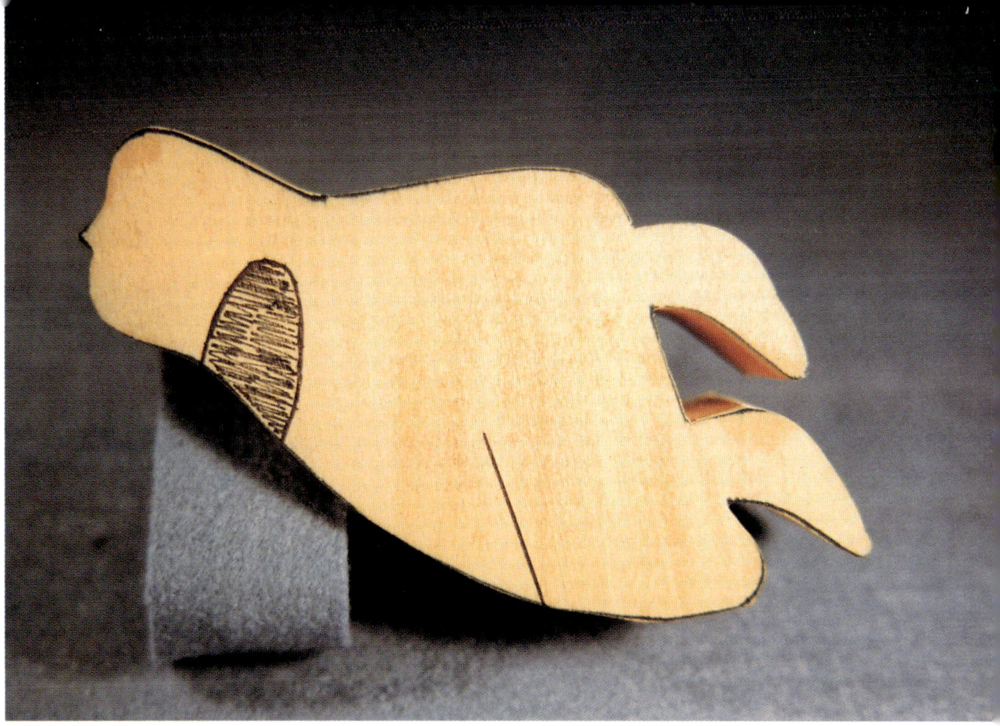

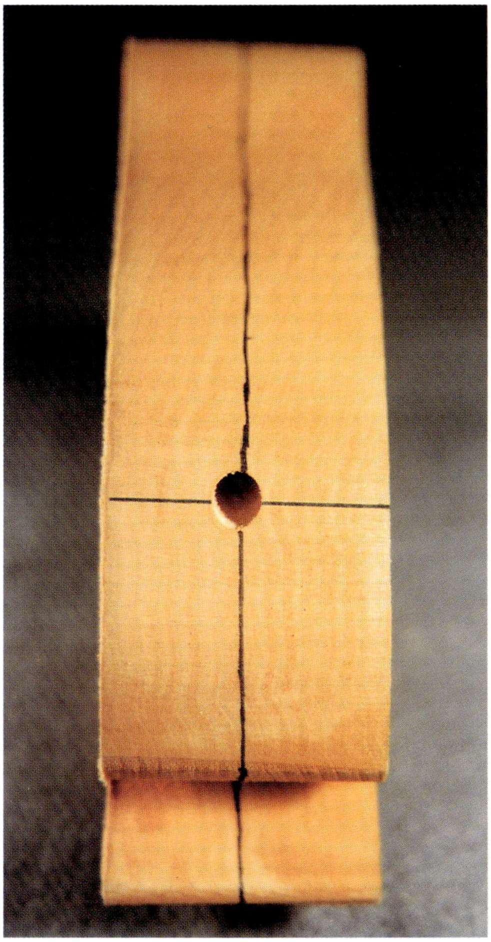

To help maintain symmetry, sketch a line approximately down the center of the body, *all* the way around.

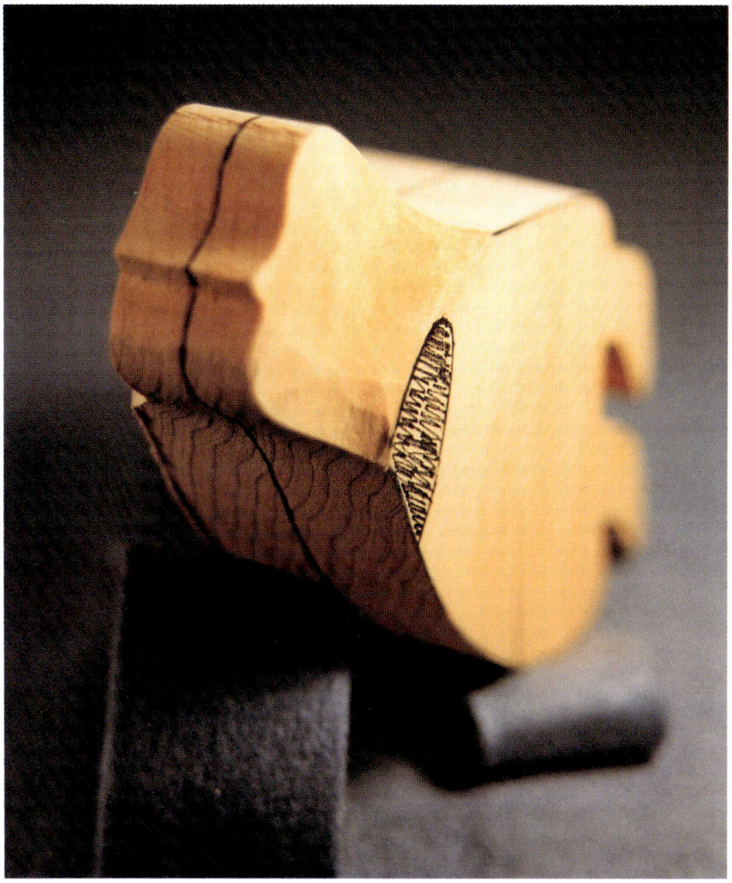

Using your knife or a flat gouge, scoop away wood from the front edge of the **"No-Carve"** zones, in order to form shoulders and reduce the width of the head. Since the grain is running vertically through the body, the wood should shave away easily. If you wish your angel to have a fat, cherubic face, only scoop away a small amount of wood. For a leaner face, remove more wood. There are no hard rules here regarding how much wood must be removed.

In order to help make your body carving easier, you may desire to clamp the larger patterns in a vise while removing large portions of wood, or when rounding the body off. This is your option, but is extremely helpful in reducing hand fatigue on the larger angels.

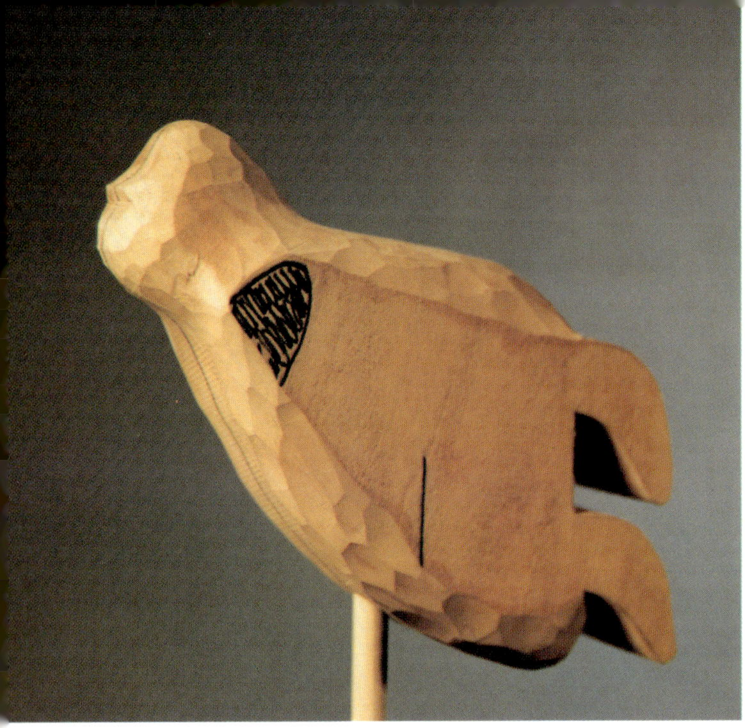

Now, using whatever method is best for you, round off the sharp edges of the body and face. Stay away from the main part of the **"No-Carve"** zones on the sides of the body. (Removing a small portion along the sharp body edges will be all right, however).

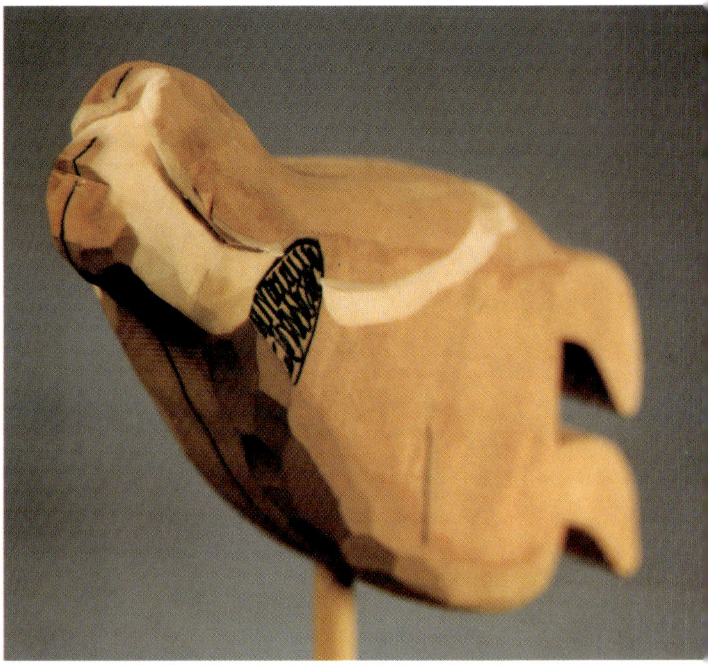

To help make the hair stand out from the face and body, remove wood from the face by shaving **UP** and **BACK** toward the hair. Remove wood from the body by shaving from the body **TOWARD** the hair all around, as appropriate. We'll do more work on the hair in a later step.

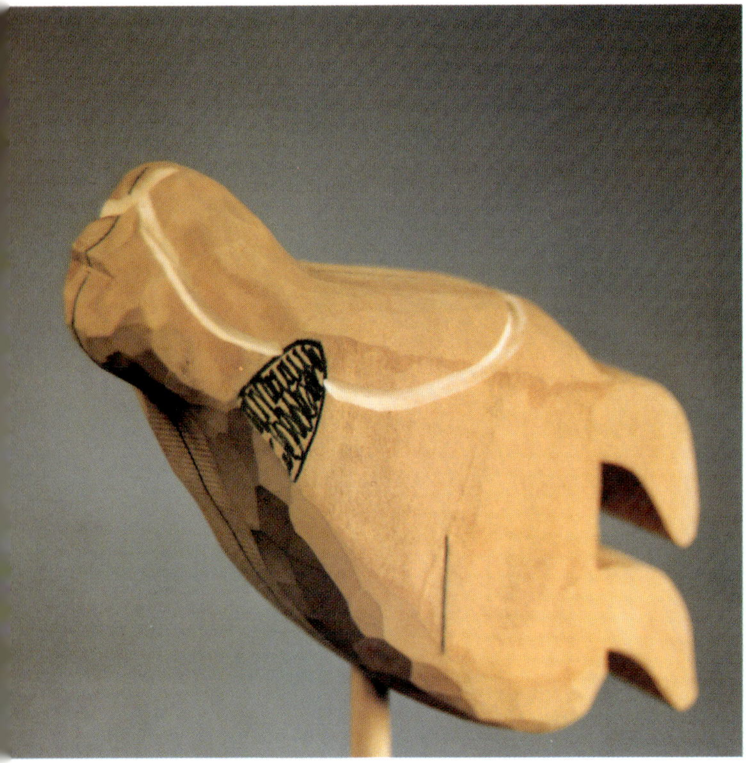

Sketch the outlines of the hair. Incise these lines with your knife tip, or go over them using a **1/4" V-gouge**.

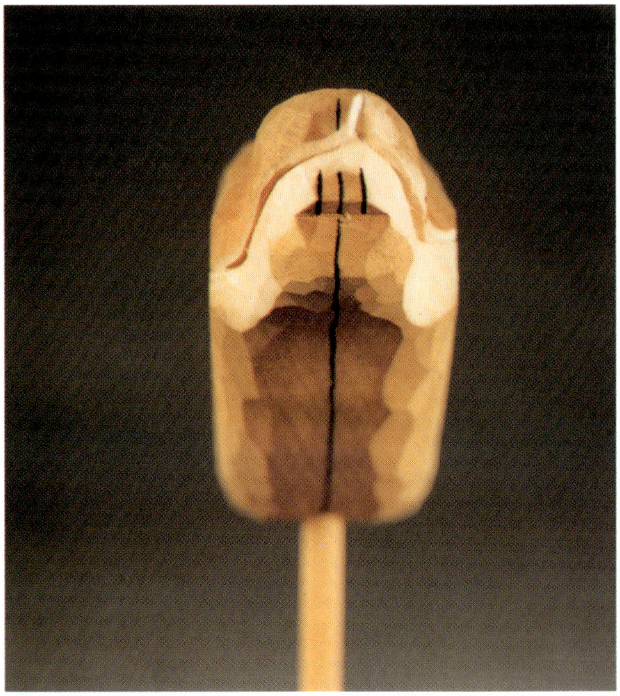

Let's start detailing the face by establishing the nose width. Sketch vertical lines up the nose as shown. This is another flexible area. You can have a wide nose or a narrow nose, or anything in between. Whatever you decide, sketch the nose a little wider than you want to end with. (You can always remove more wood, but it's real hard to add the wood back on).

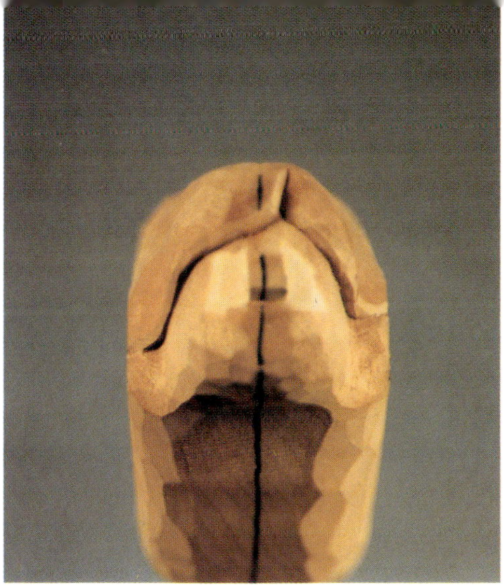

Use your knife to remove the excess sections of wood from each side of the nose. Then use your knife to round off any sharp edges on the face produced by this step.

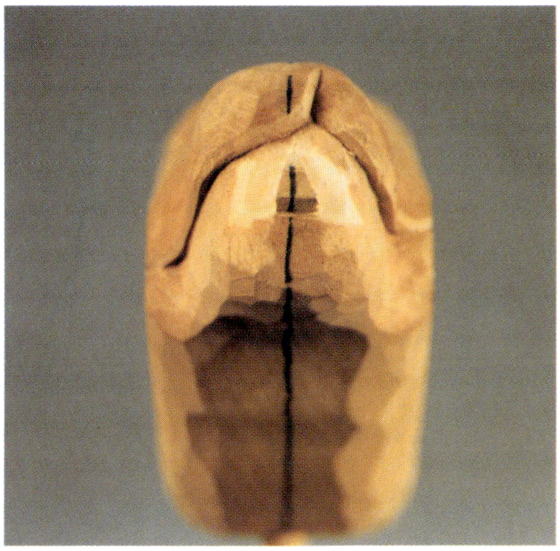

Now, incise from the bottom corners of the nose up to the top center of the nose, and remove this wood, leaving a triangular shape for the nose.

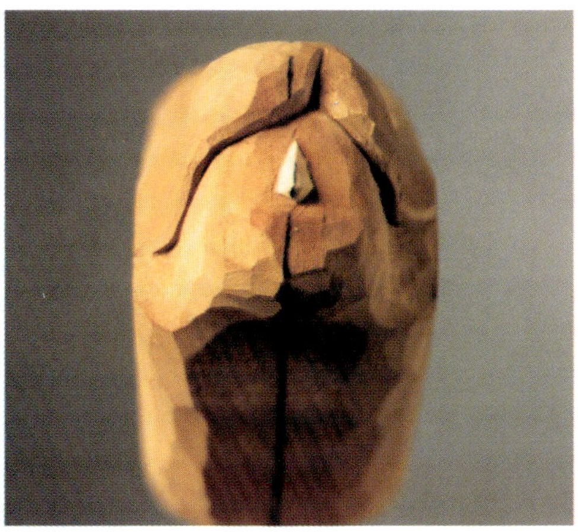

Use your knife to round off any remaining sharp edges on the nose, and clip off the lower outside corners of the nose at about a 45 degree angle. If you desire to make the nose thinner, now is the time to do it. We will add a bit more detail to the nose in a later step.

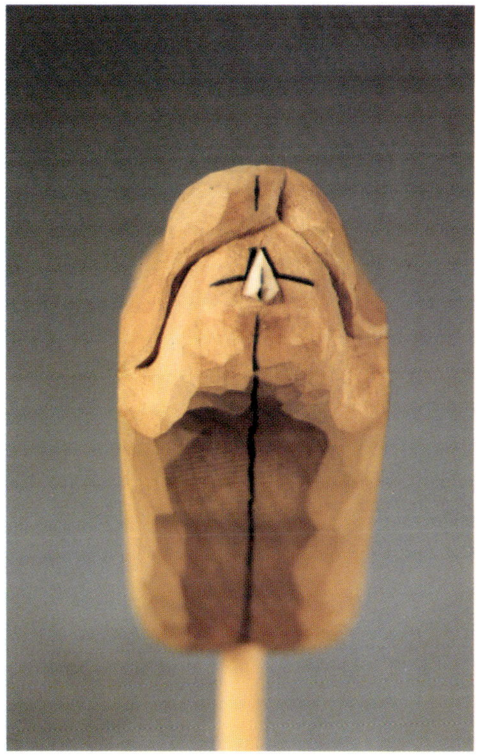

Sketch lines up the sides of the nose and across the cheeks to define the inside edge of the eye socket, and the lower edge of the eye socket (upper part of the cheek).

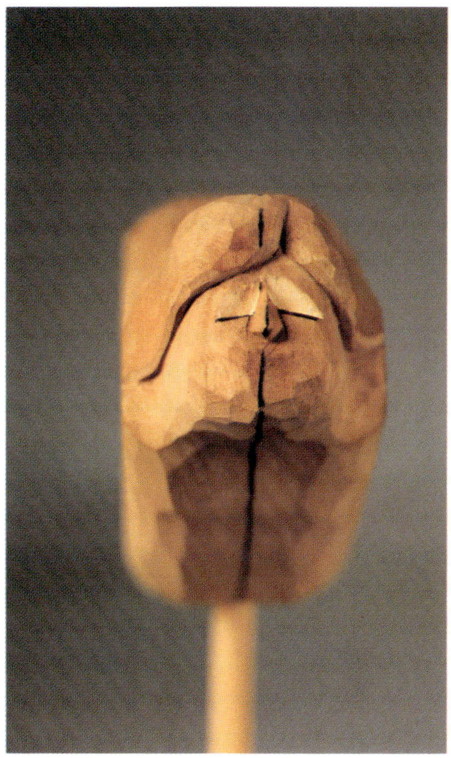

Incise these lines approximately 1/8" deep with the tip of your knife. Then, shave down from the top of the face and in from the sides with your knife. This will pop a wedge of wood loose on each side of the face, forming eye depressions. (This method works well on other forms of caricatures, also).

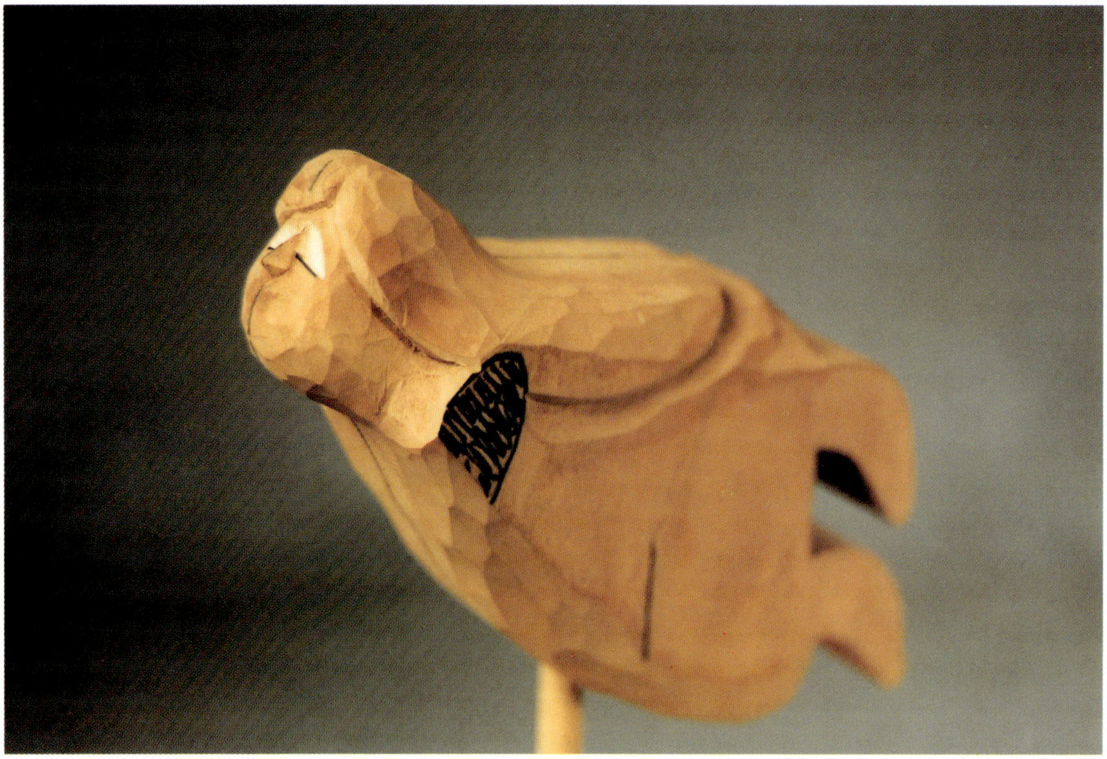

A view of the eye sockets from the side.

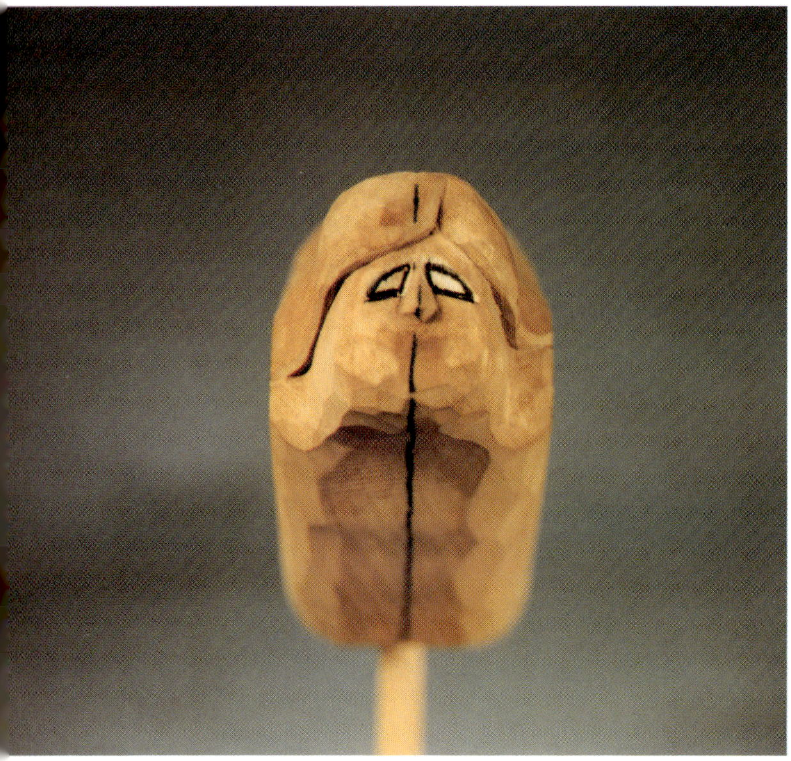

Sketch in the two eyes as indicated. These are folk-style eyes, so they are not as detailed as those on full caricatures, but they work well on carvings of this type, and look better than eyes which are just painted on.

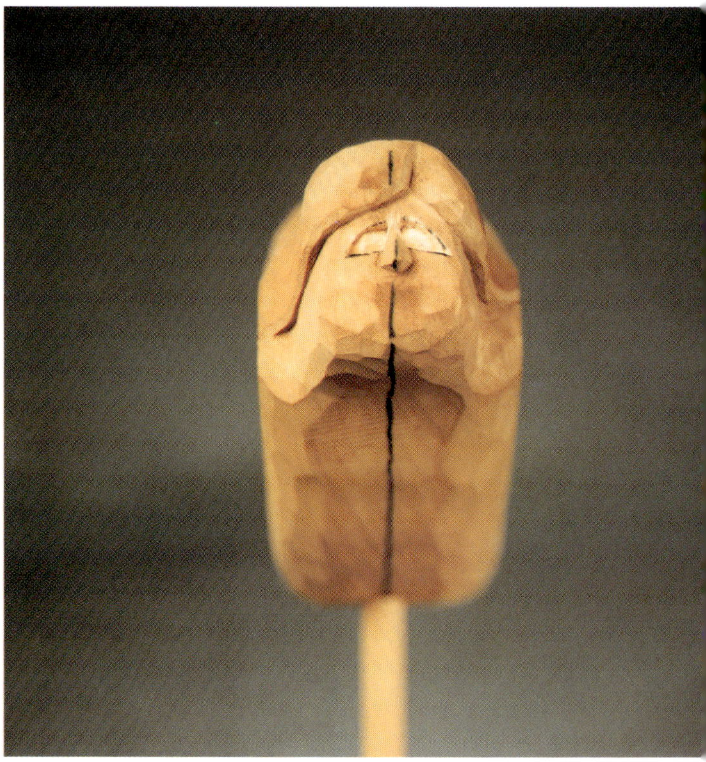

Incise all around the lines with the tip of your knife. Next, working from the *center* of each eye, shave toward the incised lines all the way around in order to remove a small amount of wood and form the eyeballs. After the eyeball is defined, you can use your knife tip to remove the sharp edges from the eyeball if you want a smoother look.

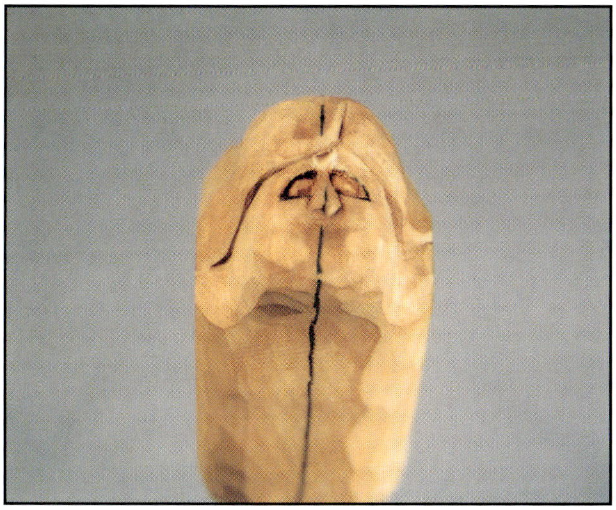

Now use a **3mm #11 gouge (Veiner)** to remove a small amount of wood from between the eyes to suggest an eyebrow separation.

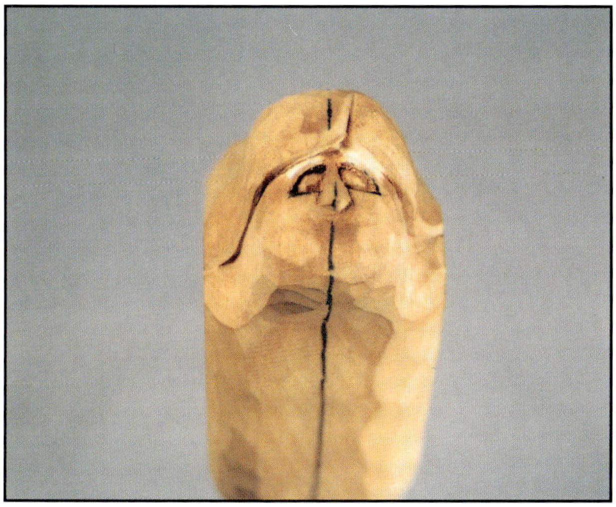

Using the tip of your knife, scoop away a slight amount of wood above the eyes, to complete the definition of the eyebrows.

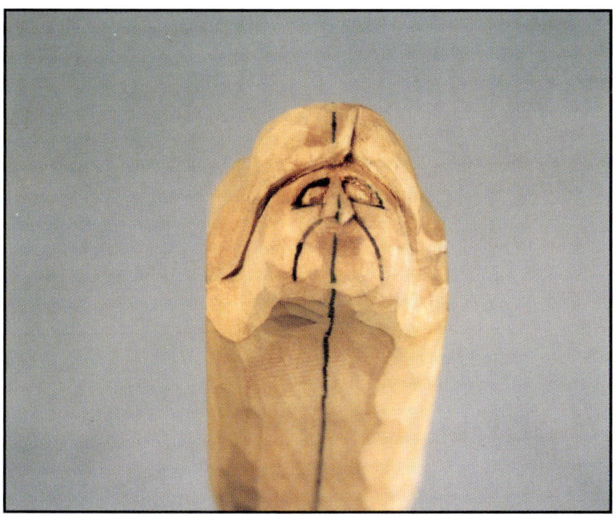

Starting from the lower outside edges of the nose, sketch lines down the cheeks as shown, to define the cheeks and form the mouth mound.

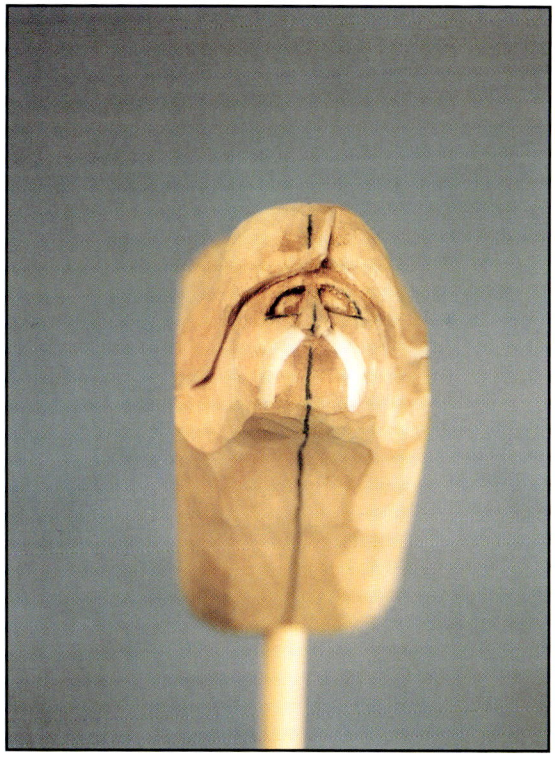

Go over these lines using the **3mm #11 gouge (Veiner)**.

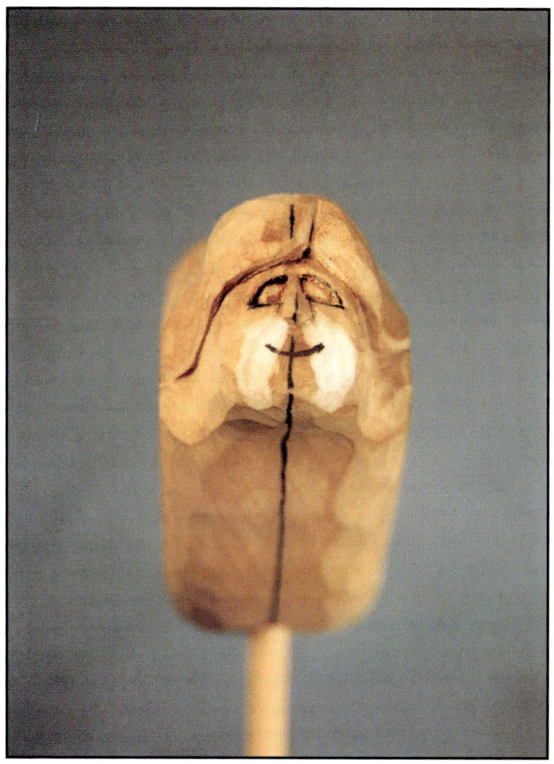

Round off any sharp edges this last step produced, then sketch in the smile line.

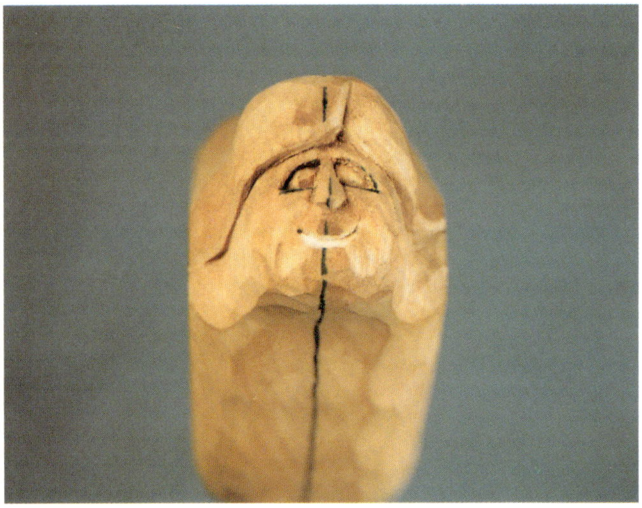

Incise the smile line with your knife. Lightly shave toward this line downward and upward to form the separation between the upper and lower lip. (A slight v-shaped channel should be the end result). You may also wish to use a **1/8" V-gouge** for this step, if it is easier for you.

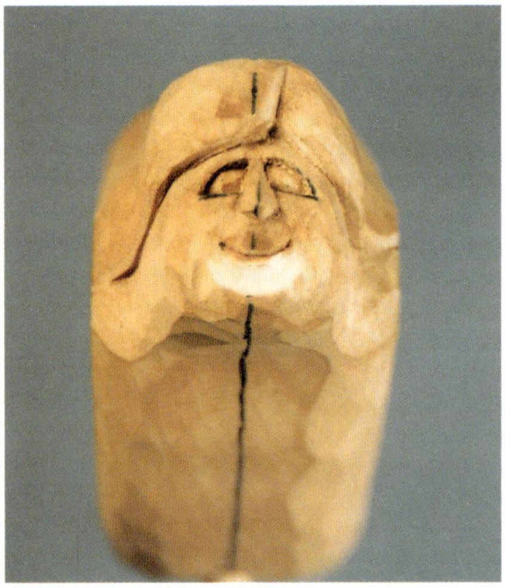

Next, use the **2mm #11 gouge (Veiner)** to remove wood from the bottom of the lower lip by cutting sideways and up toward the corners of the mouth, working from the *center* of the face toward the edges of the mouth.

Continuing to use the same gouge, cut from the *center* of the face and downward on both sides to form the chin.

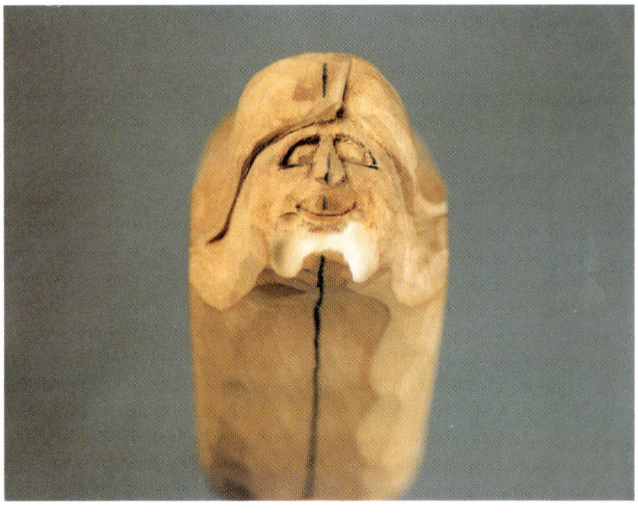

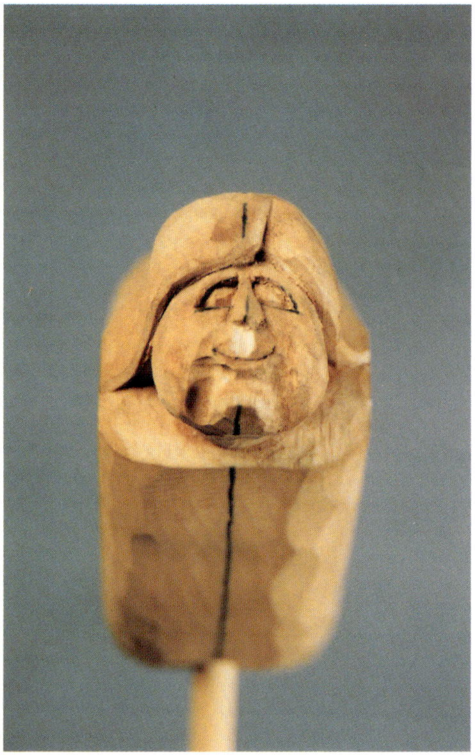

Now use the **3mm #11 gouge** to form the "angel's thumbprint" on the upper lip, and use the **2mm #11 gouge** , or your knife tip to make nostrils in the bottom of the nose.

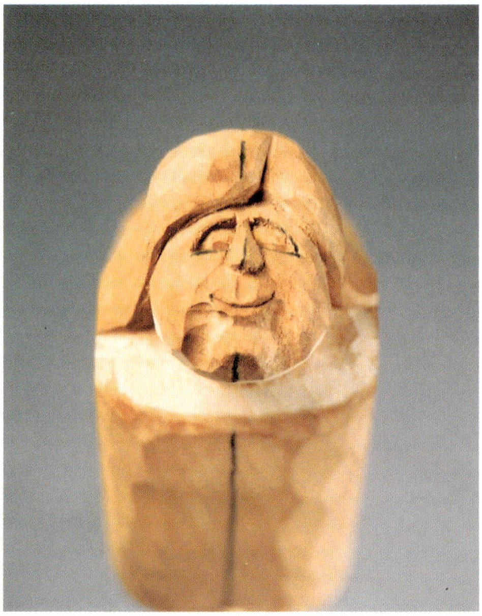

Use your knife or a gouge to remove wood below the chin and jaw so the neck area will be slimmer than the face. This is a judgment call on your part. You can remove only a small amount of wood to merely suggest a neck, or you can remove a large portion of wood to produce a more pronounced neck. This is another variable that you can change from one carving to the other.

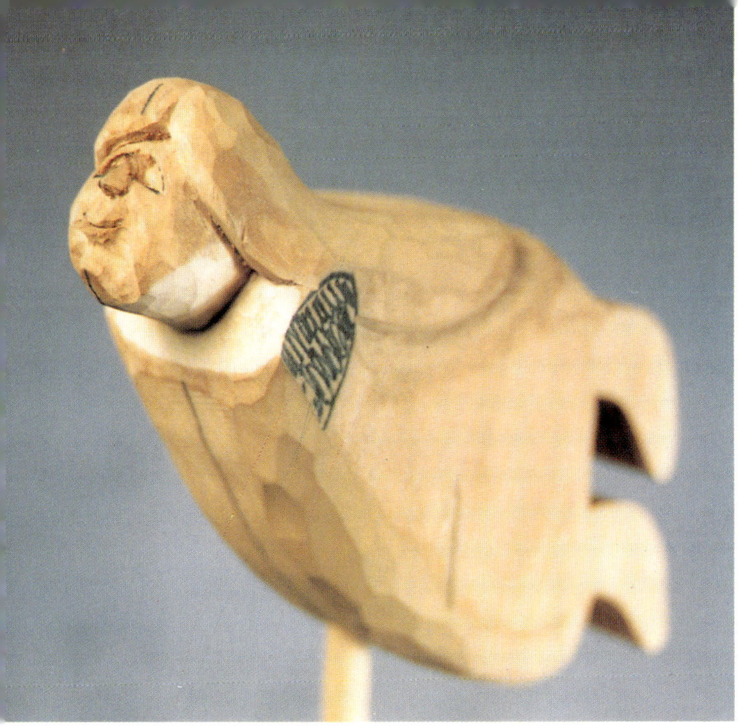

Another view of the jaw and neck. At this point we are through carving the face details. Check for symmetry, and correct any areas that don't look right to you.

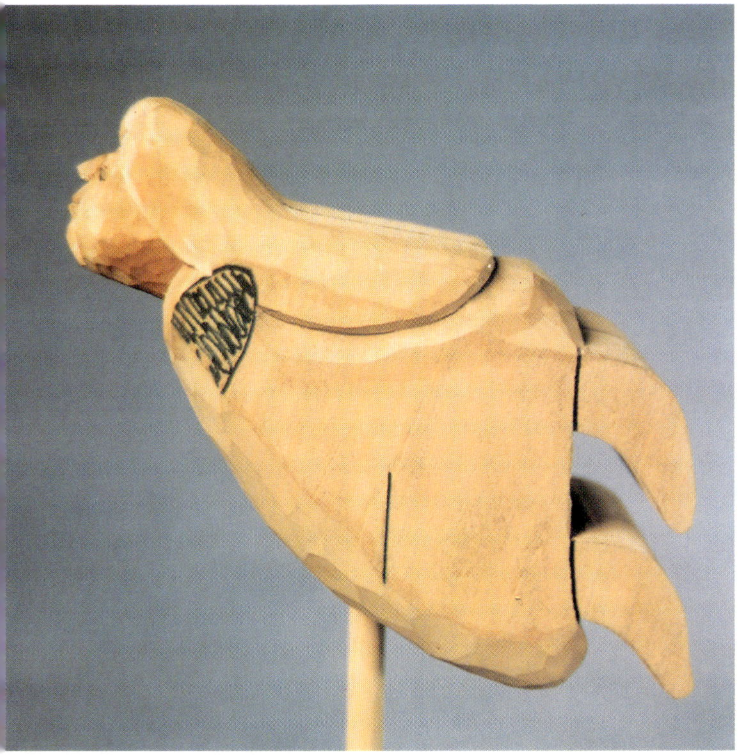

Sketch lines on both sides of the body to define the separation of the robe and feet.

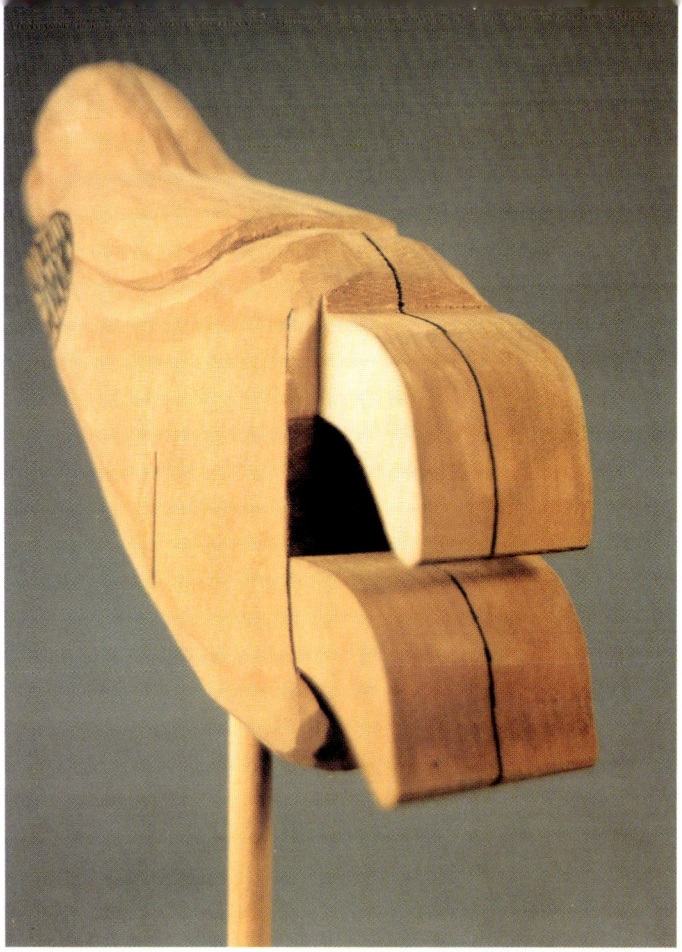

Using your knife, incise the line on the left foot about 1/8" deep. Since the grain is oriented vertically through the body, the wood will pop off easily if you slice from the bottom of the foot toward the robe. Continue doing this until you have removed about a 1/4" thickness of wood.

Turn the body over and do the same thing, continuing to incise and slice until you have removed wood down to the centerline you sketched on the body previously. If you wish your angel to have thinner legs and feet, just slice away more wood.

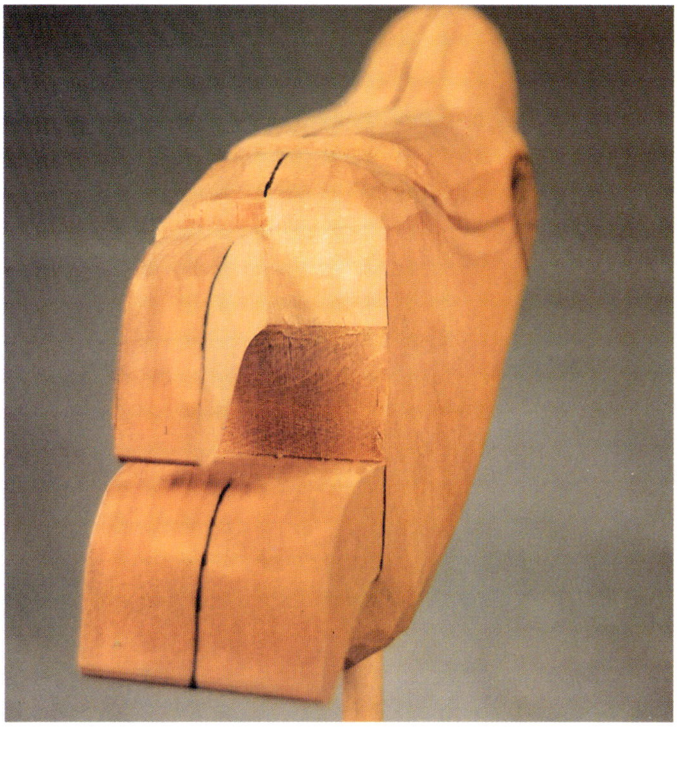

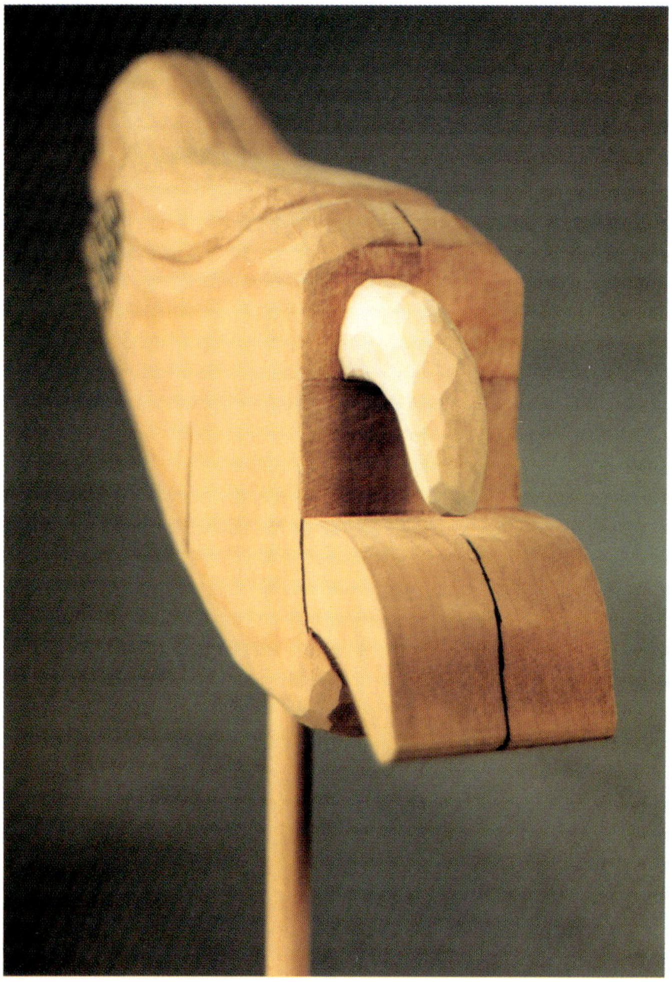

Now use your knife to round off the heel and toe area of the foot, and to remove all the sharp edges of the leg and foot.

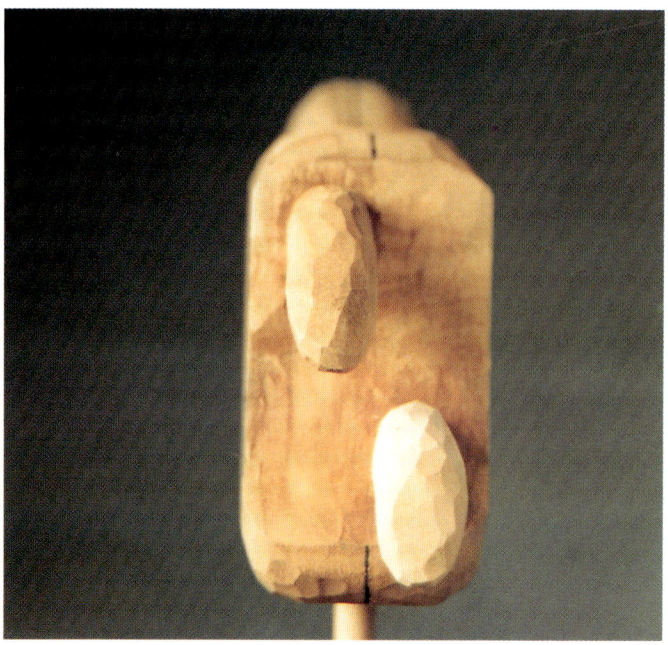

Repeat this procedure for the other leg and foot, *but be sure to locate the other leg and foot on the opposite side of the body.* If desired, you can use the **1/4" V-gouge** to cut toe details into the front of the feet.

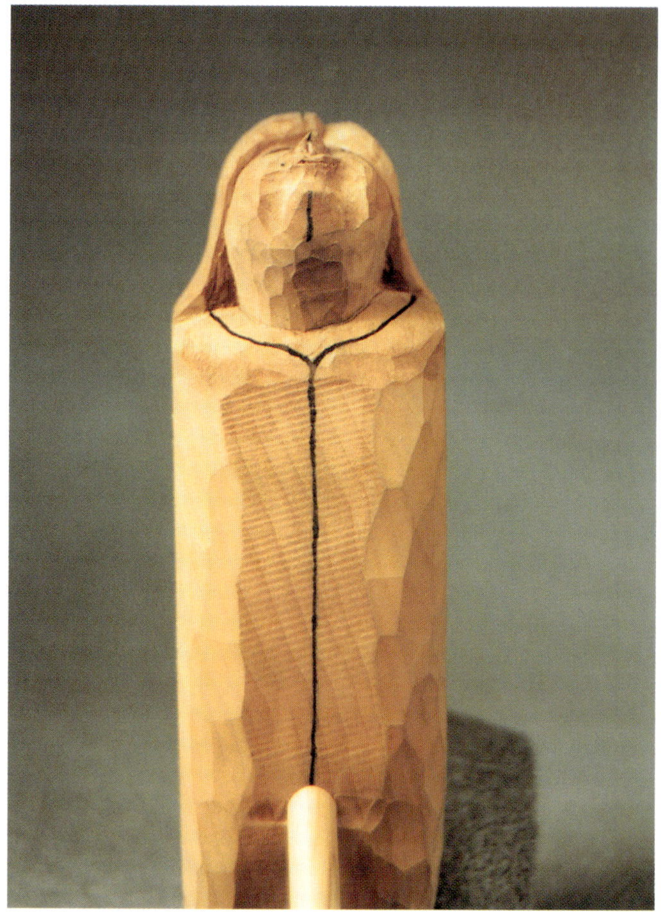

Sketch the collar and seam of the robe on the underside of the body as shown. You may use the centerline you drew earlier down the front of the body as a guideline for the seam of the robe.

Go over these lines using a **1/8" V-gouge**.

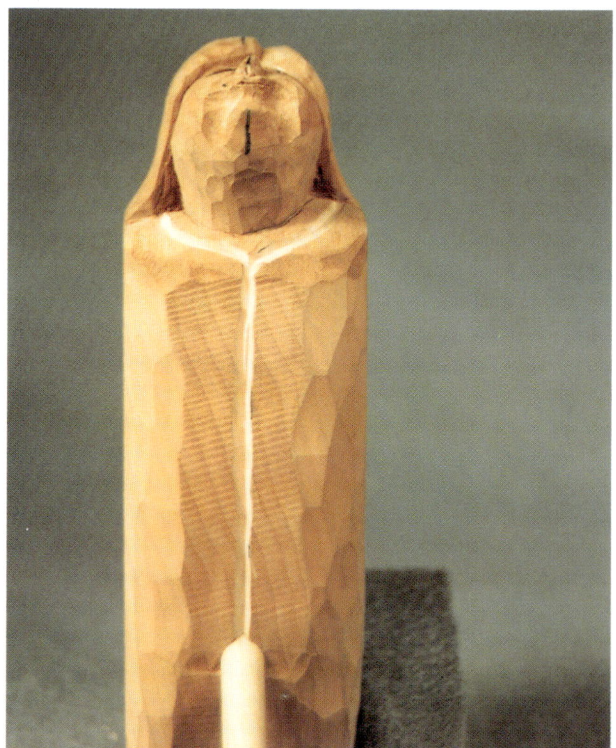

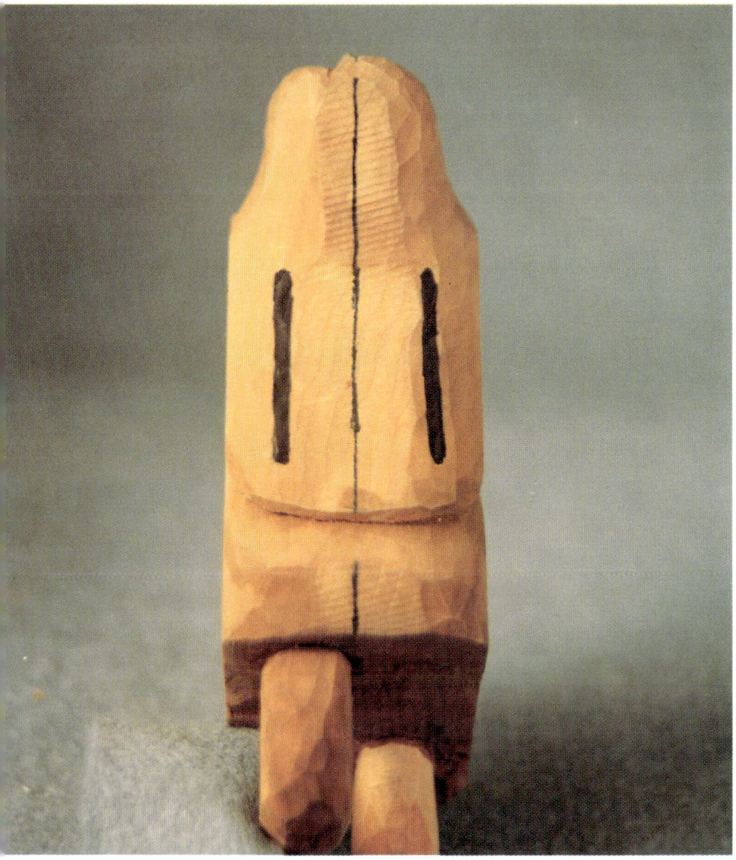

Lightly sand the wings to remove any fuzzies left by the saw. Next, hold one of the wings at a time against the top of the body as indicated by the pattern, and trace around the part that contacts the body. I usually place the wings about midway between the centerline of the body and the outer edges of the body. (The heavy dark lines in the photo indicate where I am going to remove wood to form the wing slots in the next step).

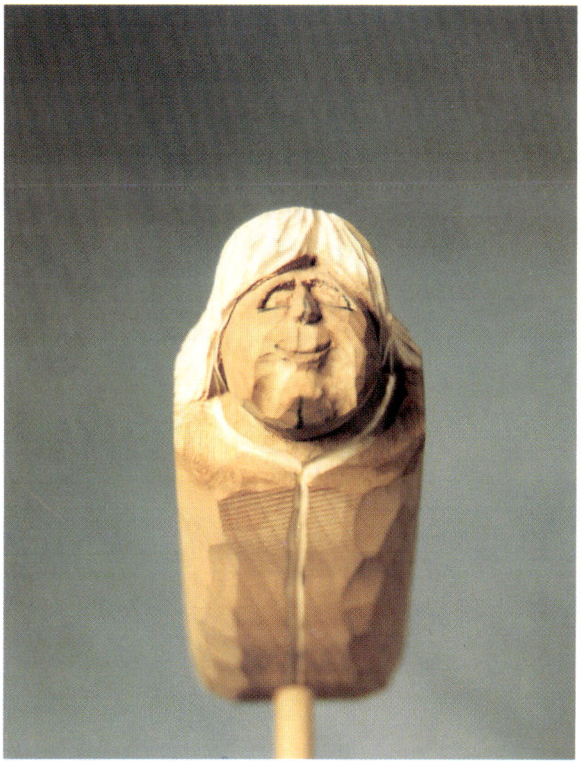

You may choose to leave the hair as it is, or detail it using V-gouges or Veiners. I added details to this angel's hair using the **1/4" V-gouge**. With practice, you can blend the hair detailing in with the wing grooves, and make it almost impossible for anyone to see how you attached the wings. Remember, do not cut into the **"NO-CARVE"** zones!

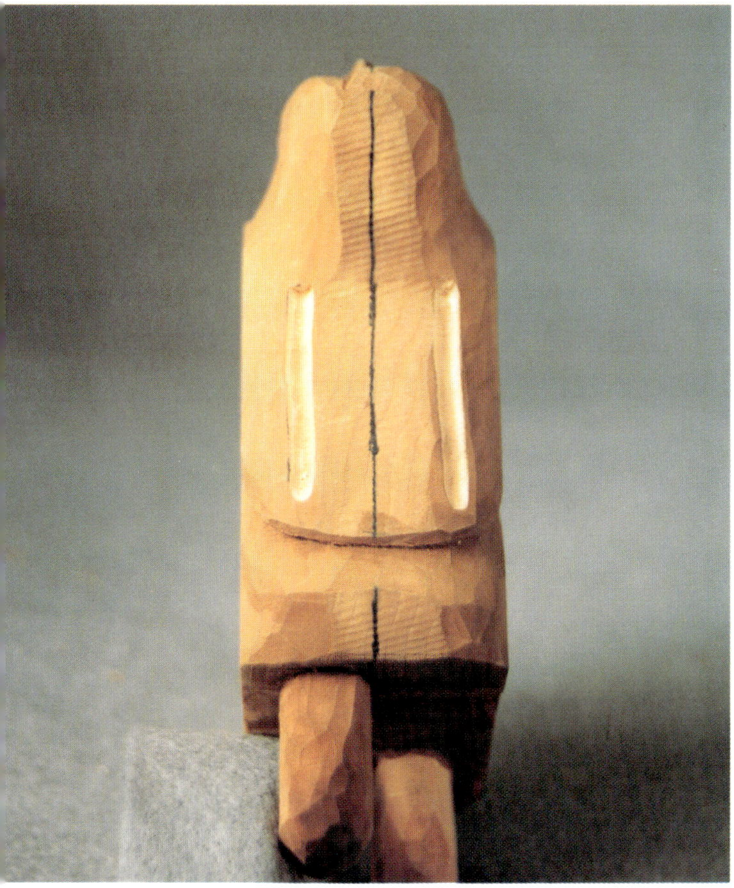

Use a **3mm #11 veiner** to cut grooves into the top of the body, following the outline of the wings which you just traced. Test-fit the wings and adjust the grooves if needed, so the wings will fit into the grooves when it is time to attach them.

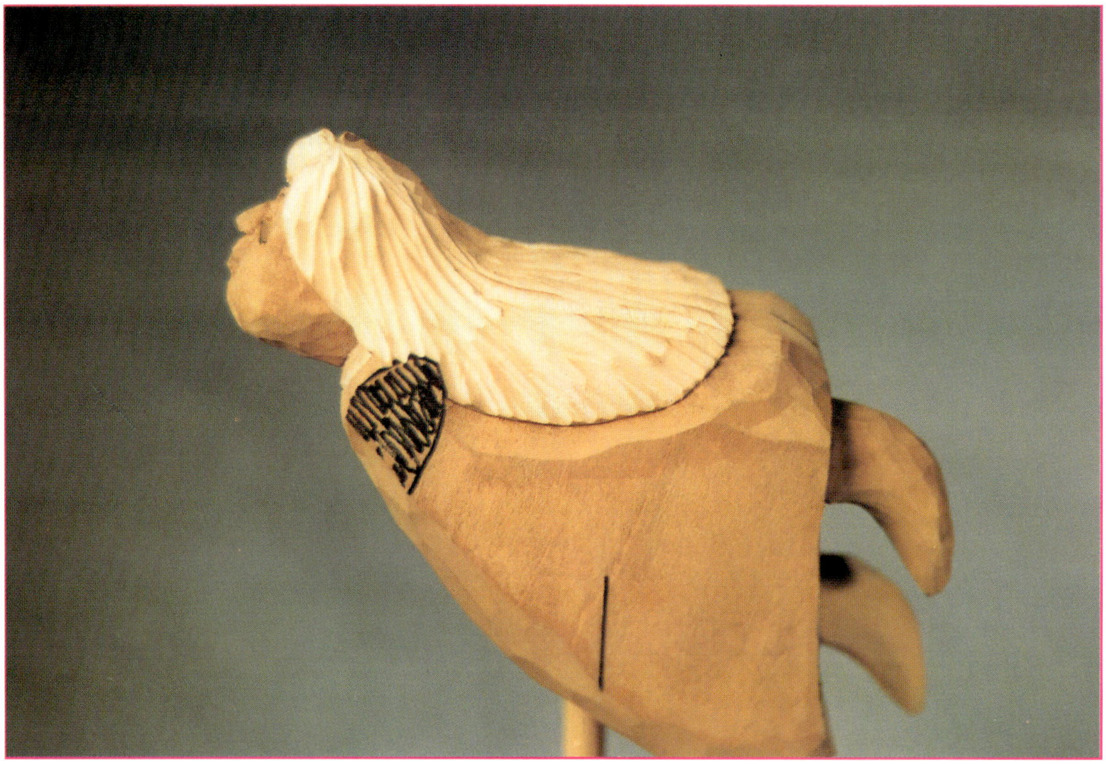

Another view of the hair details.

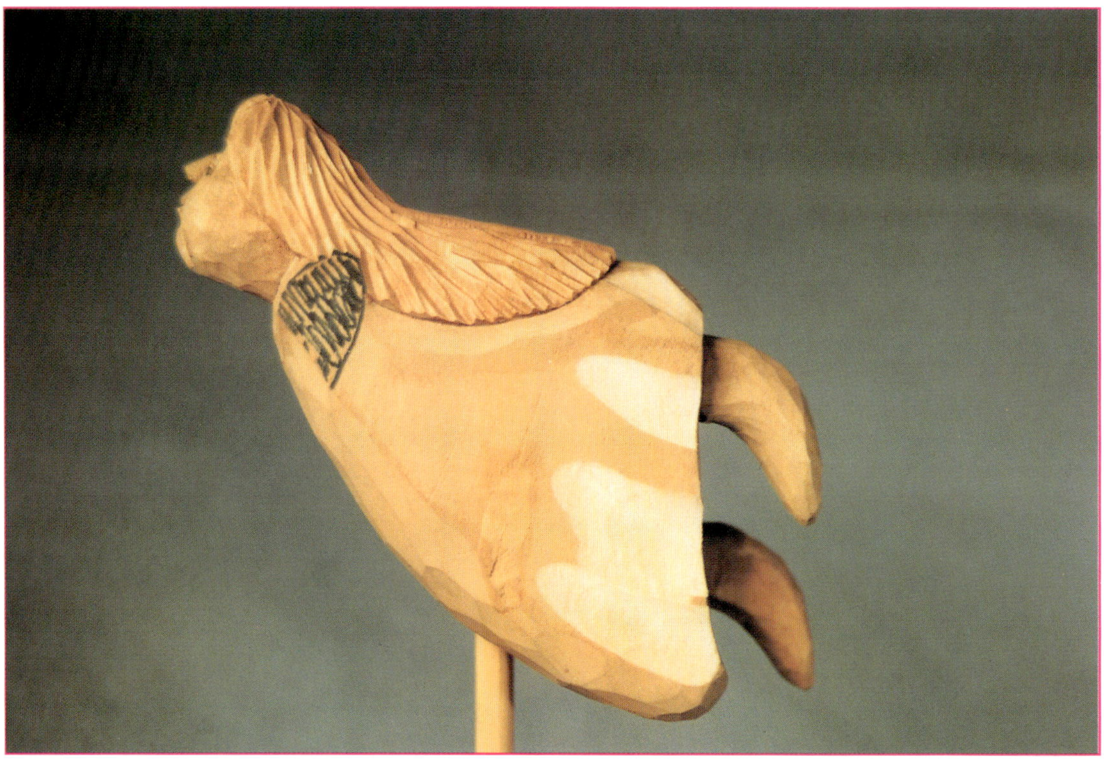

Finally, I have suggested some folds in the robe by using a **10mm #7 "U" gouge** to cut channels in the robe at random intervals, working from the rear of the robe toward the head.

At this point, we are through with the body carving for now. Look over your carving, and if there are any areas on the robe that have not been surfaced, now is the time to do it. "Surfacing" is merely a process of lightly shaving away a thin layer of wood anywhere that has not already been touched by knives or gouges, to remove any saw marks. This opens up the pores in the wood so it will accept the paint more easily and evenly.

Carving the Arms and Hands

Before we get crazy and start removing excess wood from the arms, we first have to establish some **"NO-CARVE"** zones on the part of the arms that will be glued to their corresponding areas on the body.

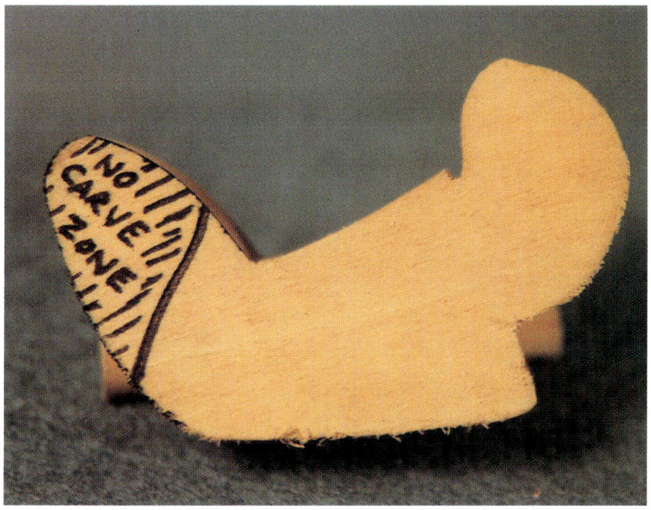

While holding the left arm in place against the body (in the **NO-CARVE** zone created earlier), draw a line on it where it contacts the underside of the body. This will define the area of the arm which must be kept flat while we round off the rest of the arm. Repeat this process for the right arm.

Now, using your knife, knock off the two sharp edges on the outside of the left arm, and also the two sharp edges on the inside of the arm (forward of the **"NO-CARVE"** zone). This should bring the arm into a hexagonal shape.

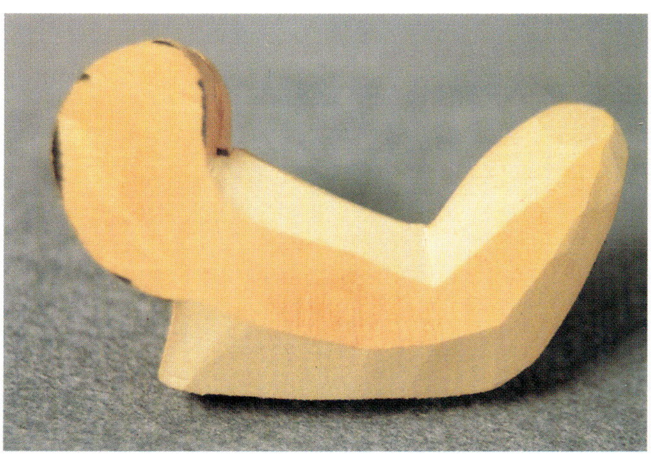

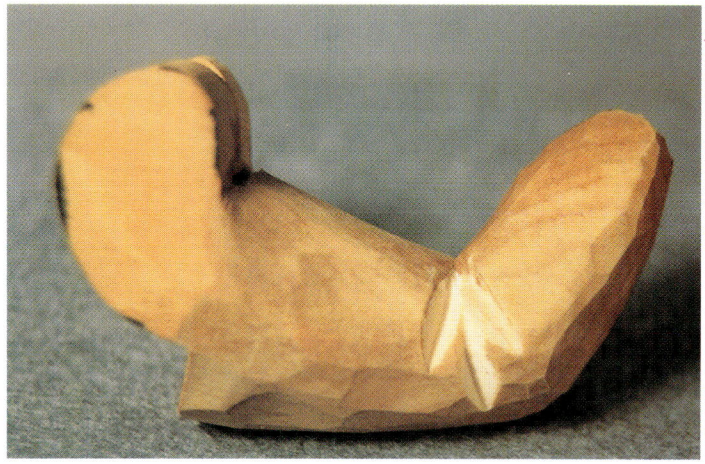

Remove the sharp edges created by this last step, and the arm should now be fairly round. I also used the **1/4" V-gouge** to add a few wrinkles in the bend of the elbow. I normally stop rounding at this point because I want to preserve some of the facets and knife cuts. This helps maintain the "hand-carved" look which people like to see.

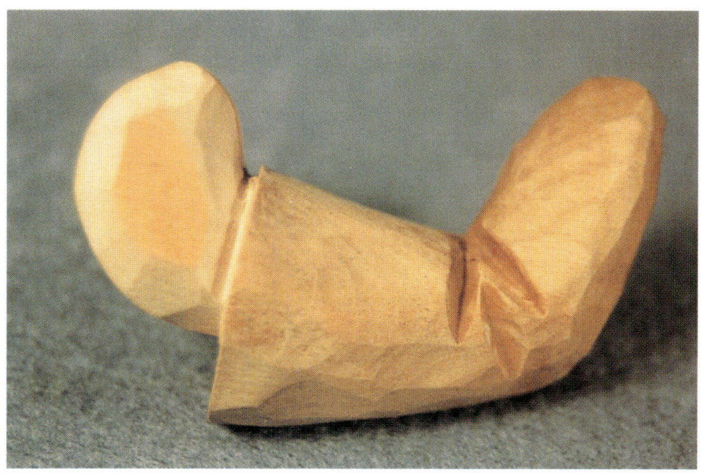

Now, use your knife to remove the four sharp edges from the left hand, and to separate the hand from the sleeve all the way around.

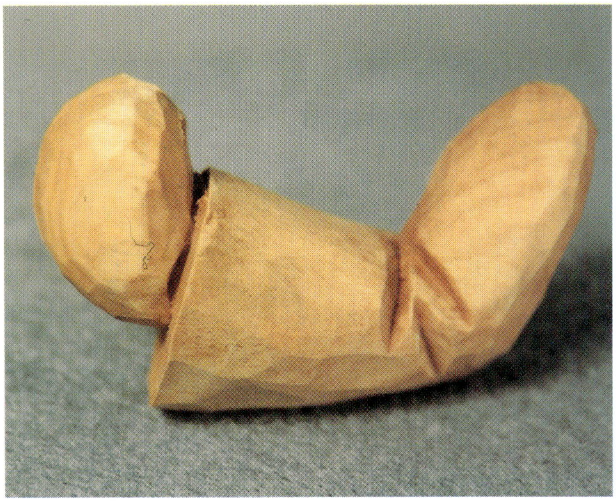

Remove the sharp edges created by the last step, and that should have us ready to finish detailing the hand.

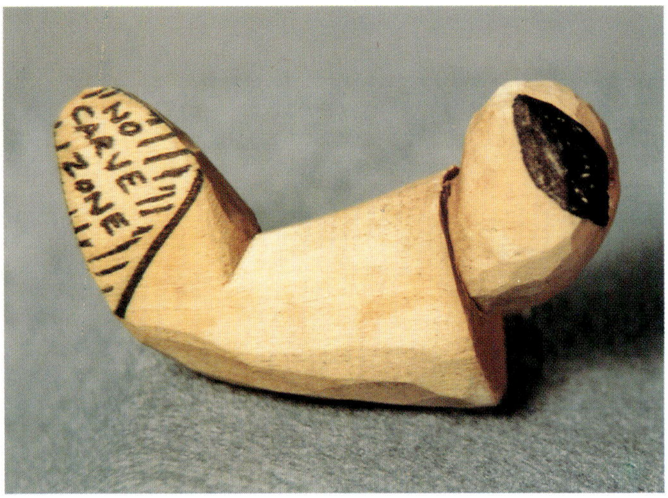

Sketch the thumb on the left hand (and wood to be removed), as indicated by the darkened area.

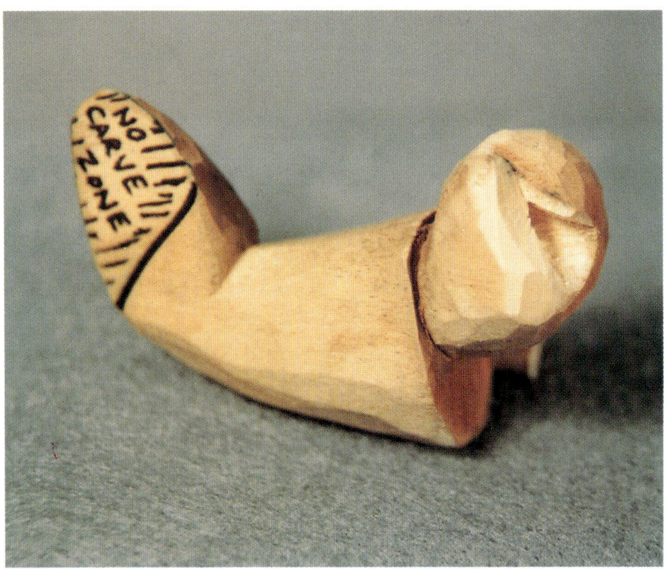

Use your knife to remove this darkened section and separate the thumb area from the fingers.

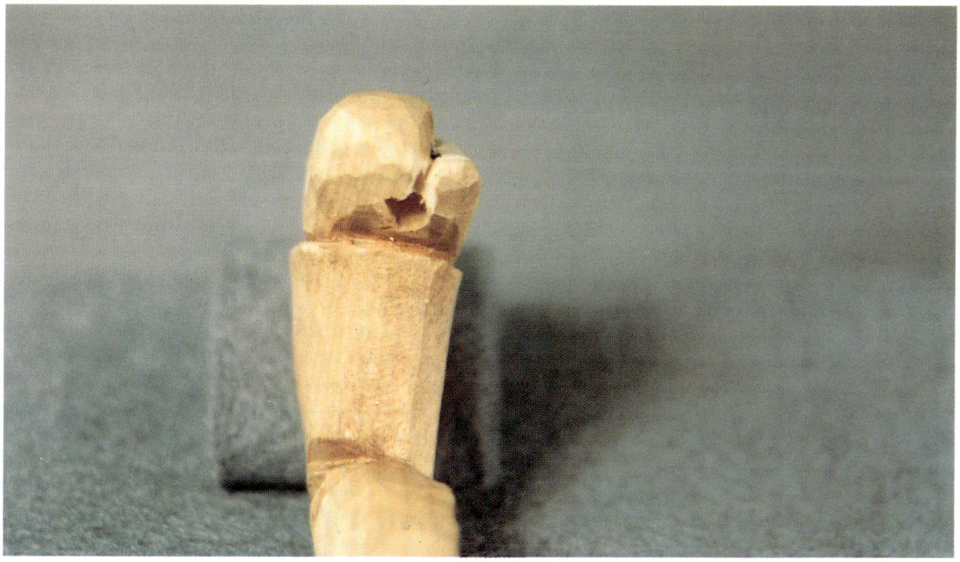

Viewing the hand from the top, use the **1/8" V-gouge** to cut a slight channel between the thumb and fingers.

Sketch the four fingers on the hand, then go over the lines with the **1/8" V-gouge** to form the finger separations. (Refer to the TIPS section regarding hand carving for instructions on how to lay out the finger divisions easily on the hand).

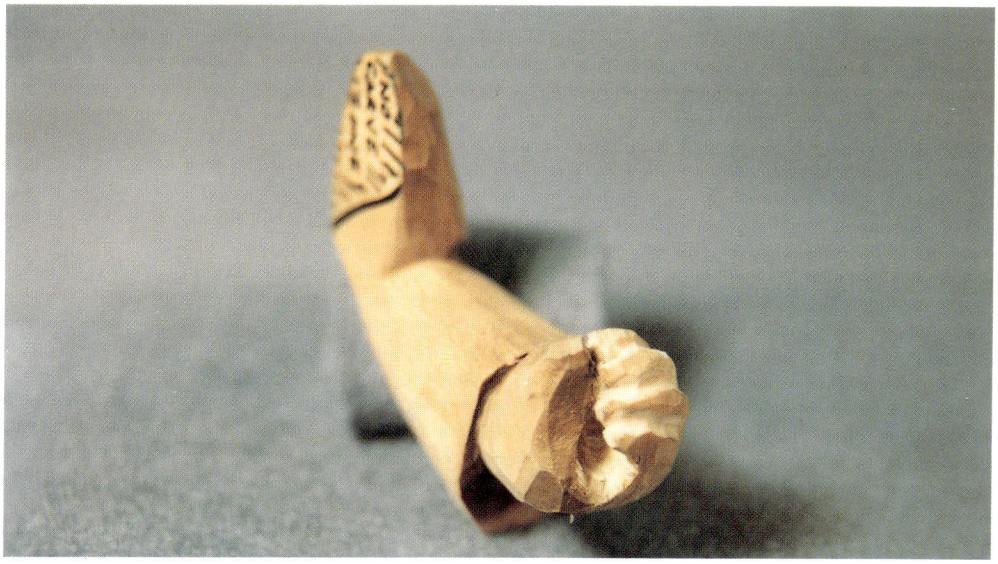

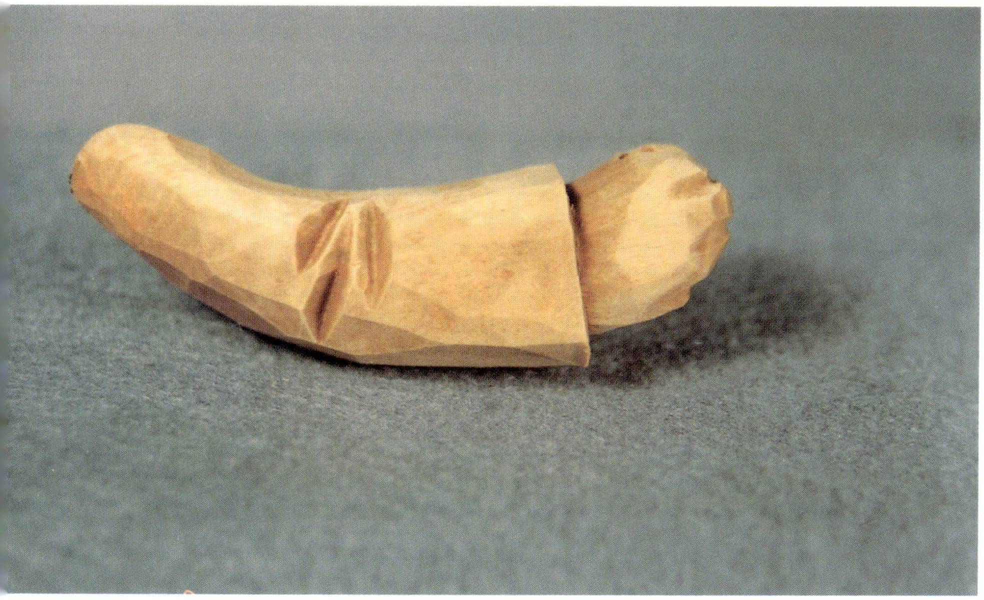

Repeat this process for the right arm and hand, and we'll be ready to continue on.

CARVING THE HORN

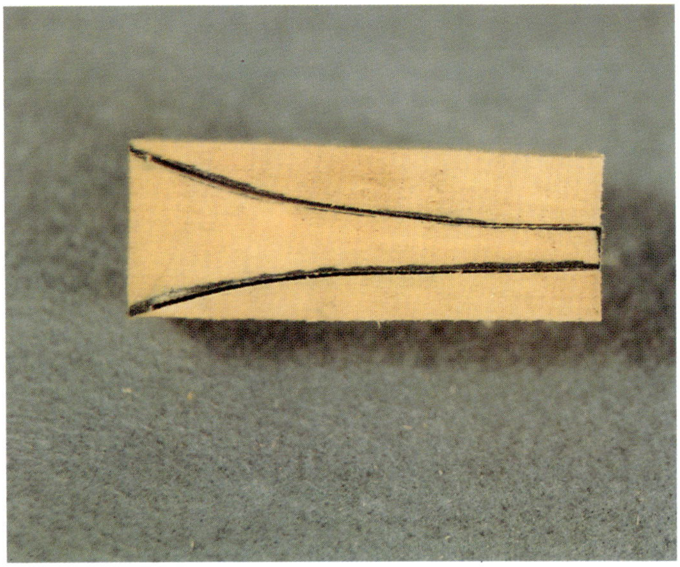

Transfer the horn pattern to the wood and saw it out. Notice that I have not cut the wood completely away from the horn at this time. We want to leave these areas flat so it will be easier to saw out the other horn profile.

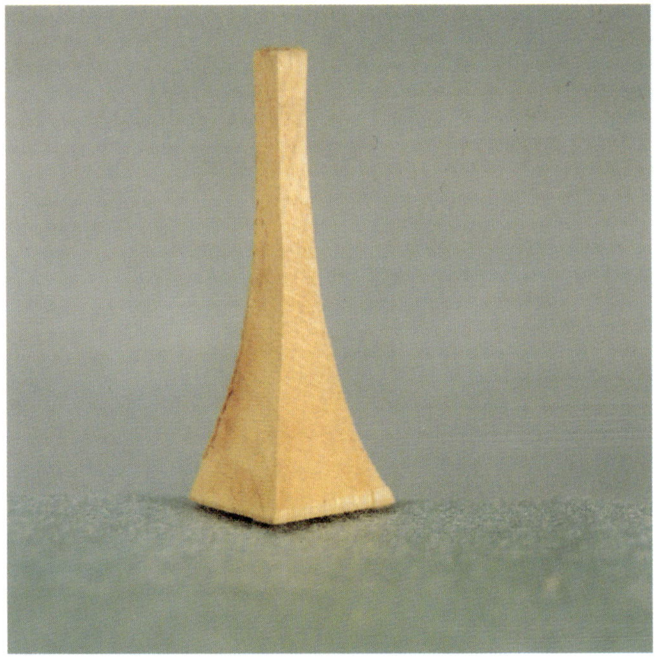

Rotate the wood 90° (on the long edge), trace the pattern again, and saw it out completely. Then saw away the wood from the first two cuts and you should now have a rough version of the horn.

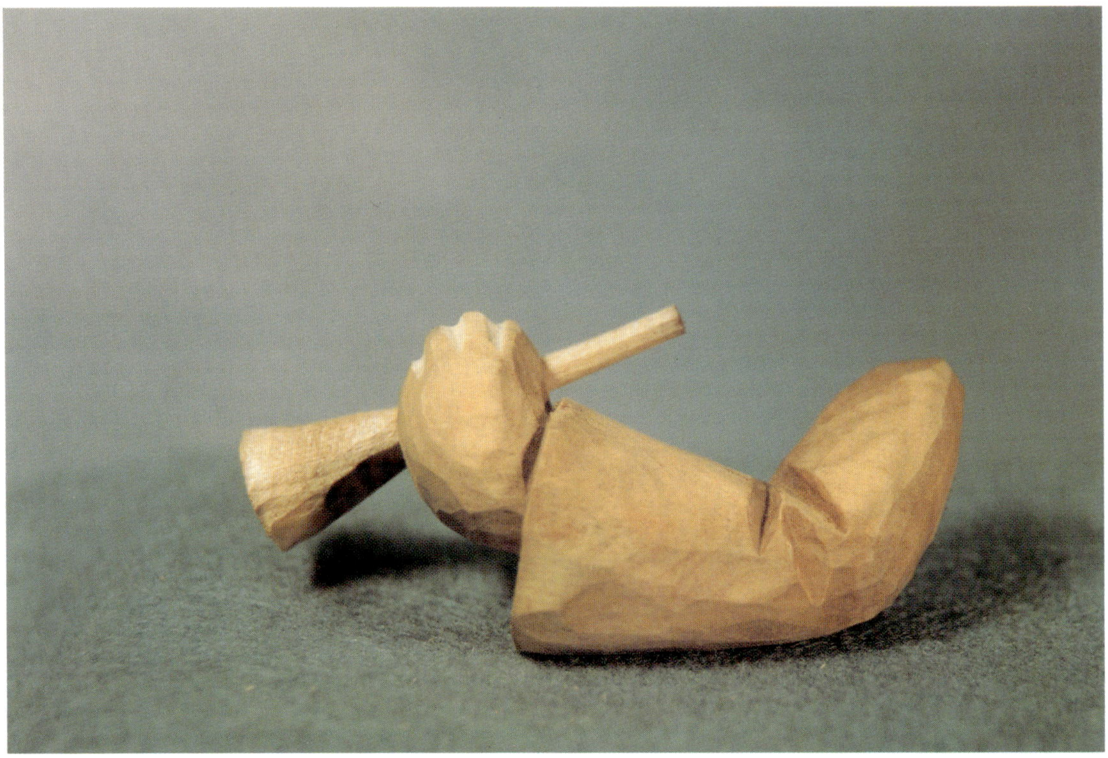

Use your knowledge of rounding to bring the horn to a finished shape. Test it in the left hand as you round it off until you get the stem of the horn to fit properly in the hole.

CARVING THE BOW

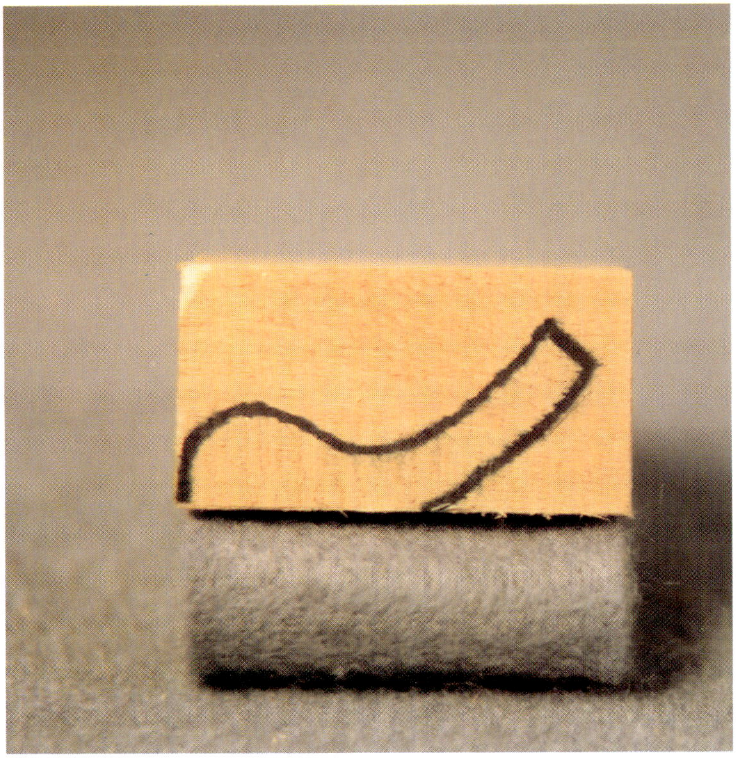

Trace or sketch the side profile of the bow on your wood and saw it out. If you have already traced it, use your saw to square up the wood.

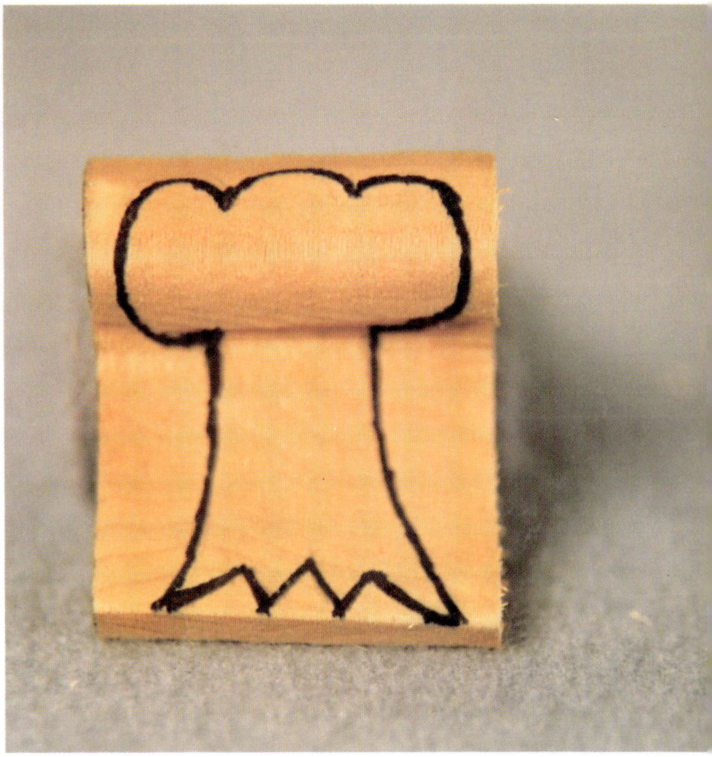

Now lay the bow flat, and trace or sketch the top profile on the wood.

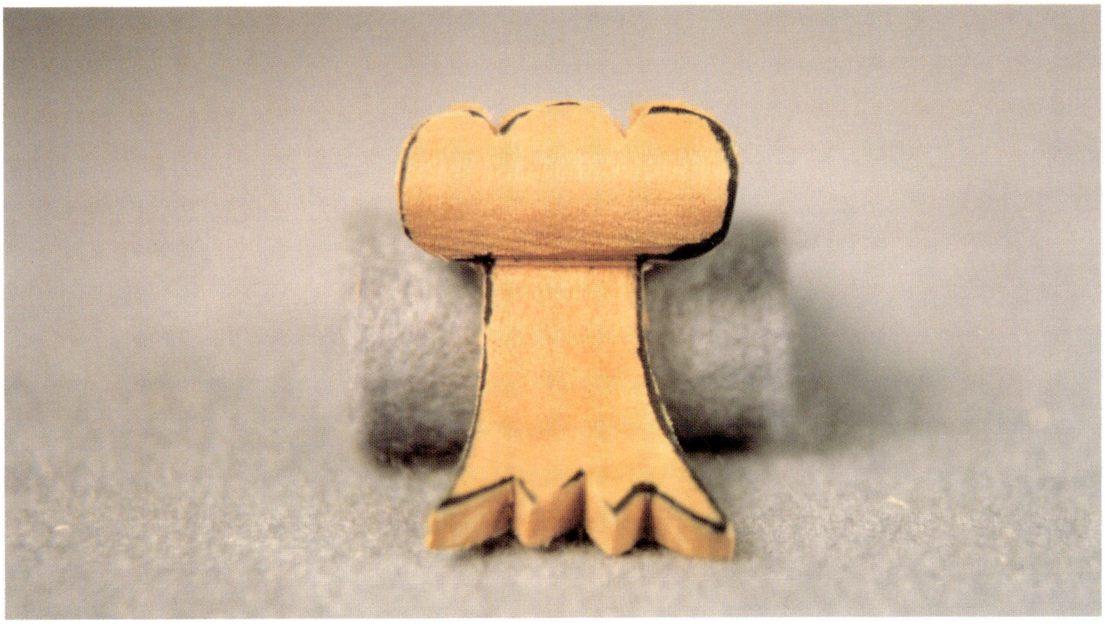

Exercise caution and saw out the top profile.

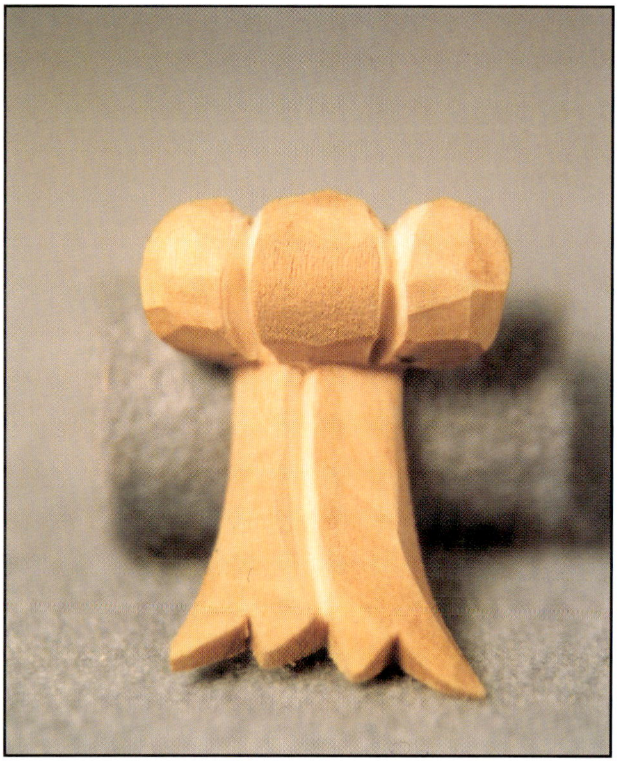

Using your knife, carefully round off all the sharp edges on the bow. Then, use the **1/8" "V"-gouge** to define the center of the bow from the two side pieces, and the streamers below the bow.

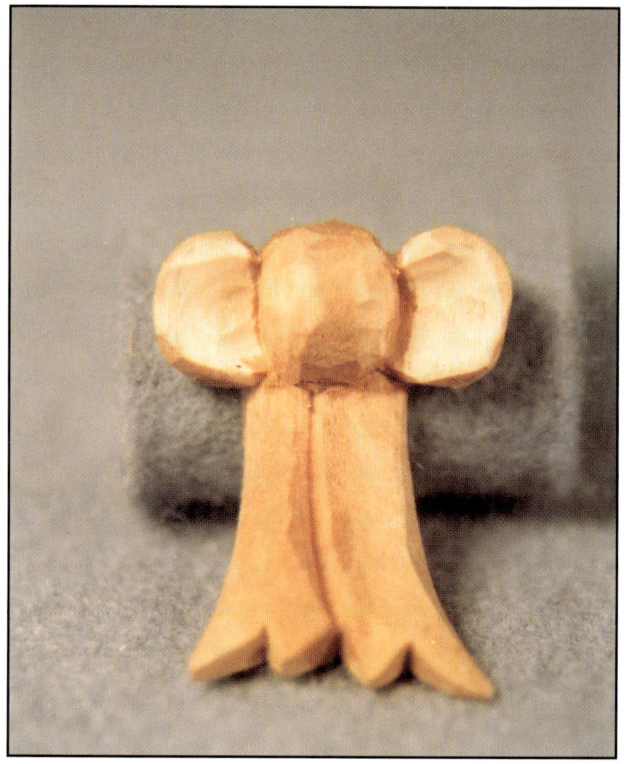

Now, using a **10mm #7 "U"- gouge**, scoop wood from the side sections toward the center section, to give a bit more dimension to the bow.

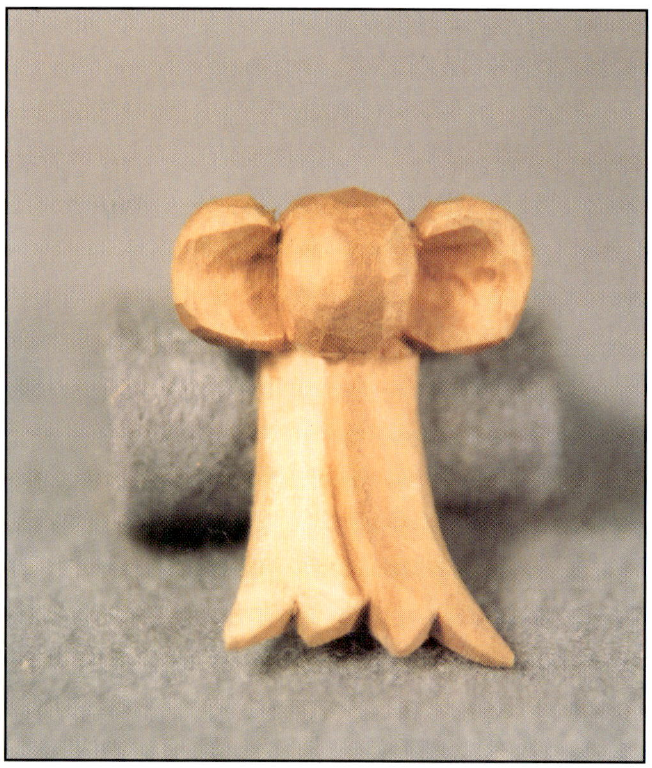

Finally, shave a light layer of wood from the right streamer so it is slightly lower than the left streamer. This adds a bit more realism to the streamers, without too much effort on your part.

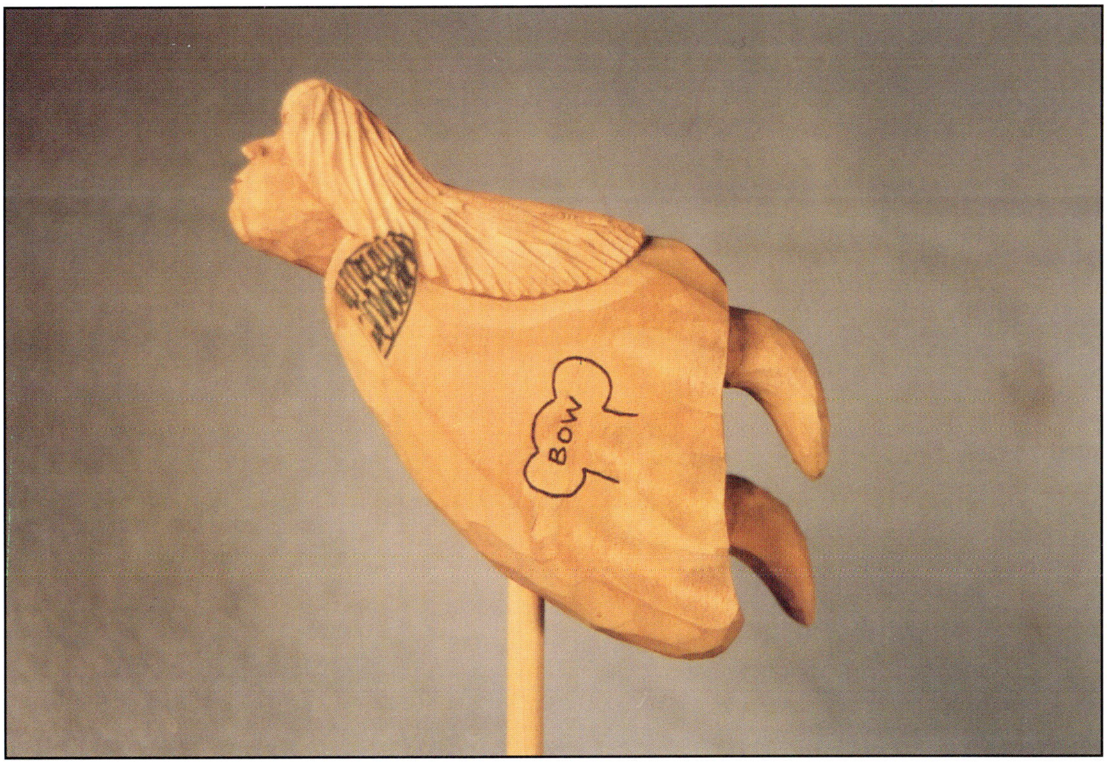

Now, hold the bow in place against the body as suggested by the pattern, and lightly trace the outline of it onto the body. This will establish another "NO-CARVE" zone.

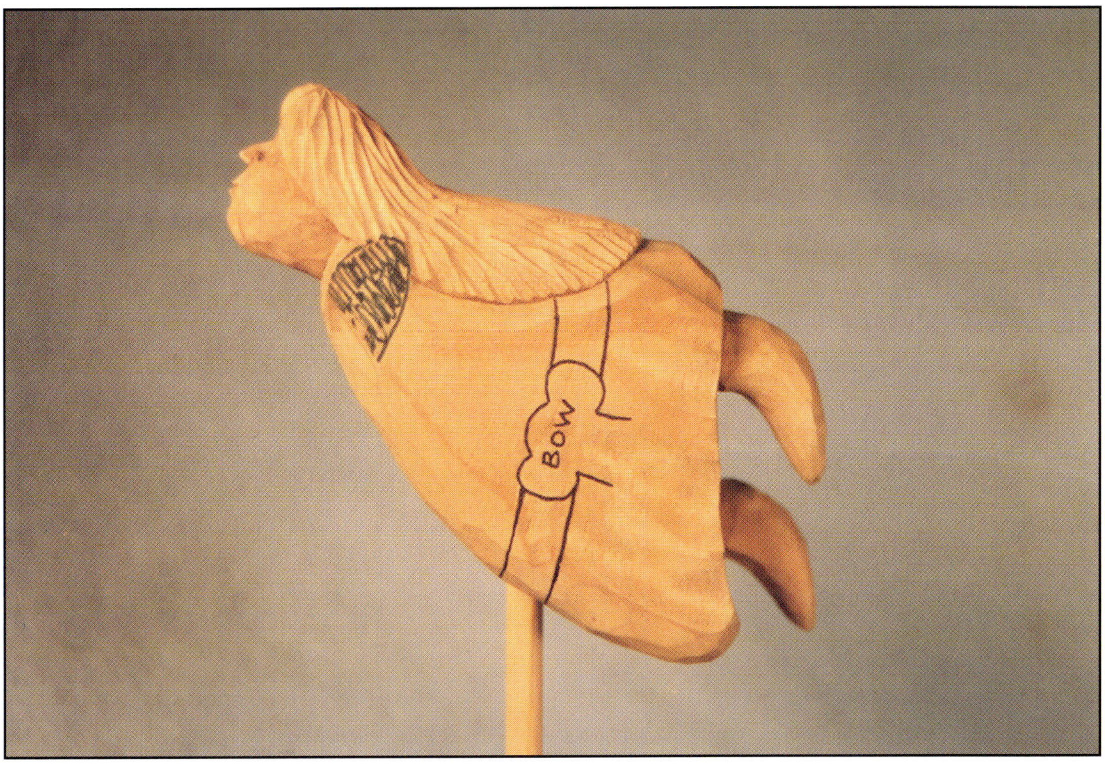

Again referring to the pattern, sketch the bow sash pieces coming from both sides of the bow. These go up the hair, down around the waist, and up to the hair on the other side. I placed the sash so it fell over the hole where the dowel for the base will be inserted later. This is an example of planning ahead, and it prevents these cuts from interfering with the seams we cut for the robe earlier.

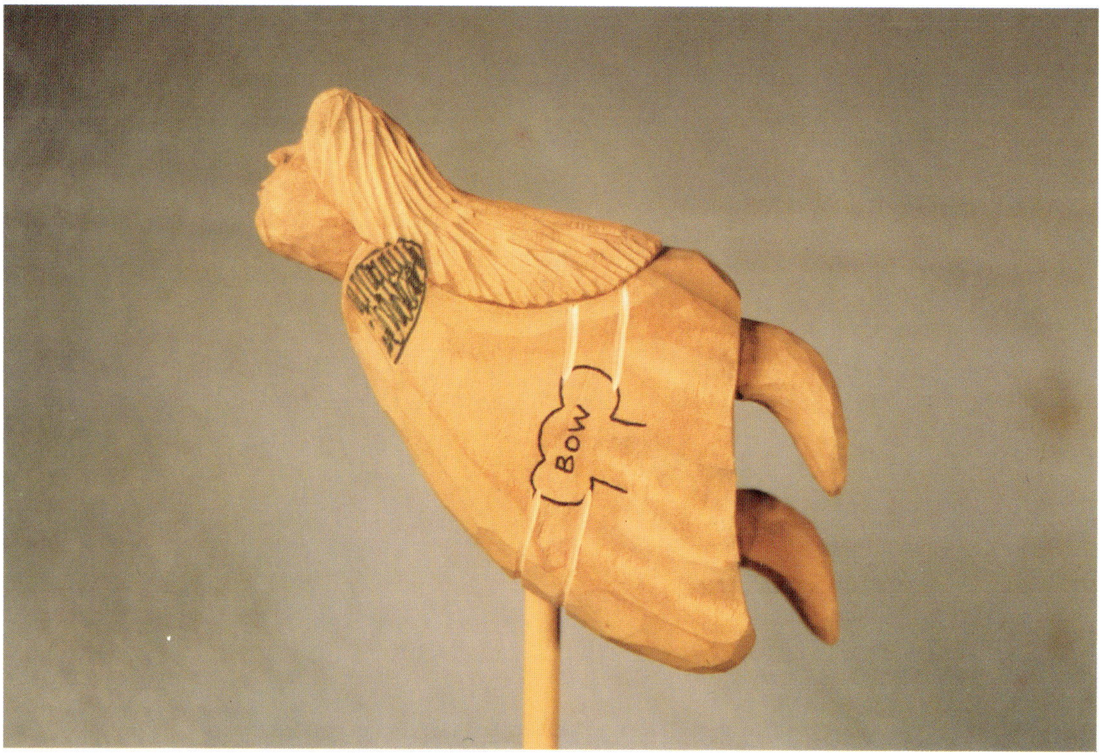

Go over these lines with your **1/8" V-gouge** to define them. (Try to stay out of the "NO-CARVE" zone, but if you should cut into it slightly, the bow should hide any transgressions when it is glued in place later).

We are through carving all the pieces. Now, a few pieces have to be assembled and finished before we start painting.

Put a small amount of glue in the grooves on the top of the body, and set the wings in place. Hold them if necessary until the glue begins to set up. Set this assembly aside and let the glue dry overnight.

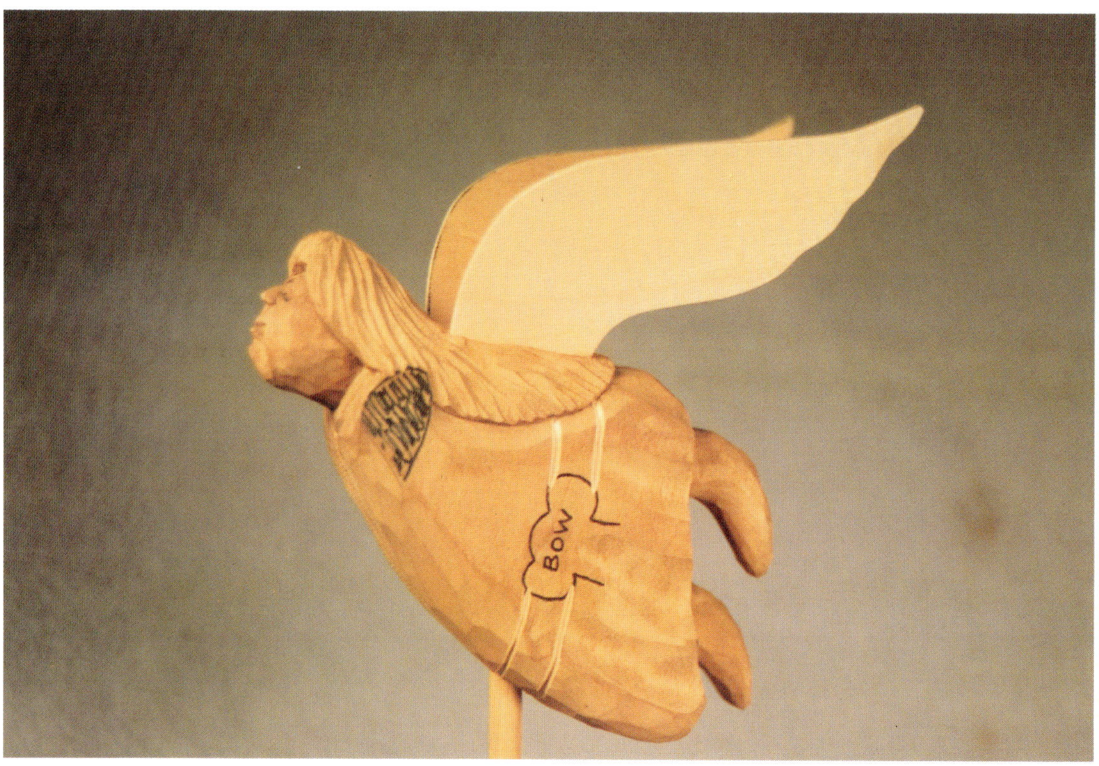

Now, if there are any major gaps where the wings join the body, they must be filled in before painting. I normally use the type of epoxy that comes in a small roll. The hardener and epoxy are in the same piece. Following the directions on the package, mix a small amount and use it to fill in the gaps where needed. It normally sets up in about 10 minutes. If you already have a wood filler that works for you, by all means use it.

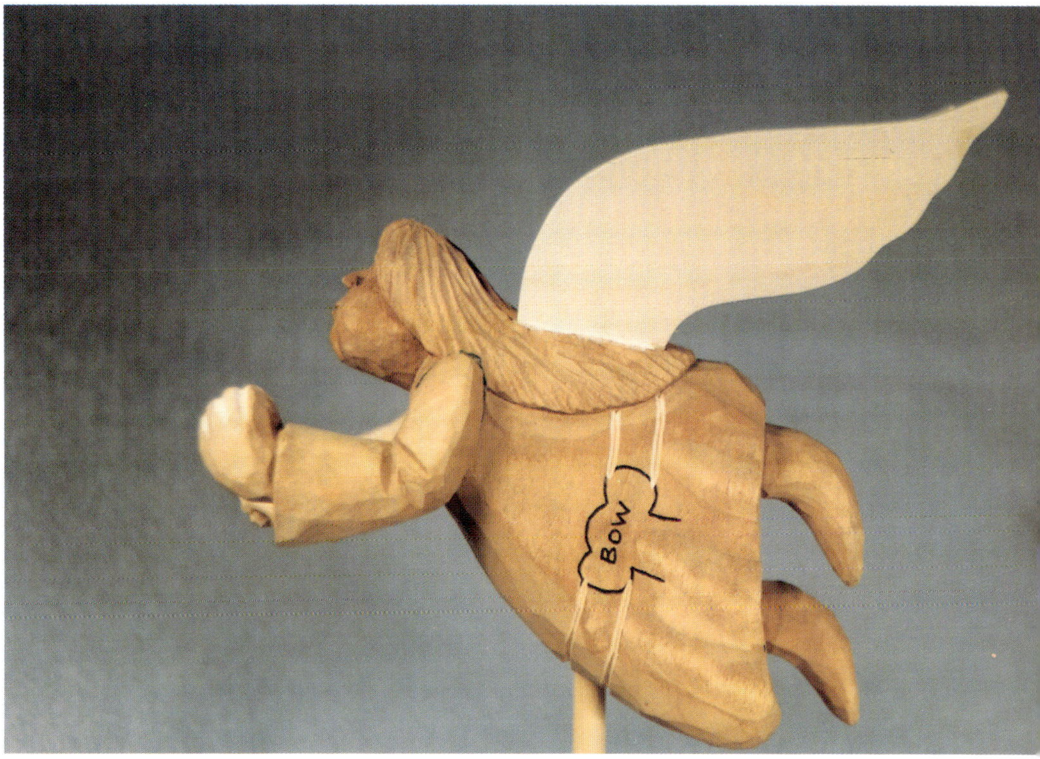

Rub a small amount of wood glue on the **"NO-CARVE"** zones on the body and arms. This will seal the wood and make a better bond. After a minute or two, put a small bit of glue on the left arm and set it in place.

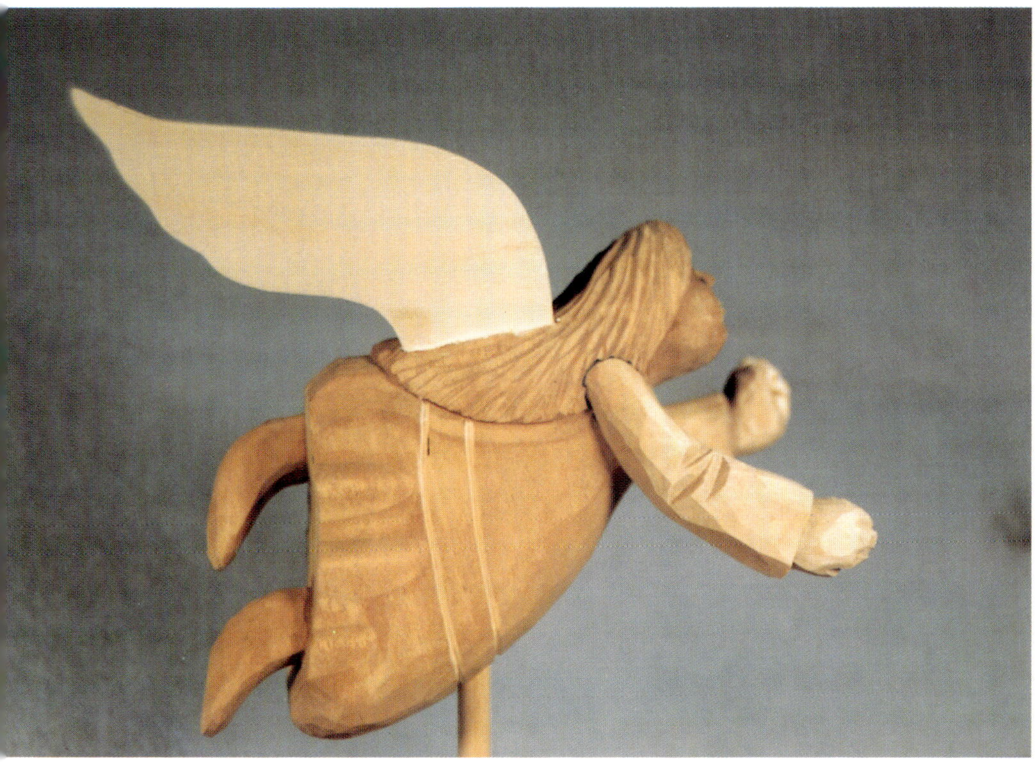

Once the left arm becomes stable, repeat the process for the right arm. Set the assembly aside and let the glue dry for at least 8 hours.

PAINTING THE PROJECT

NOTE: I used full-strength paint on this angel. Because I stained the wood to make it show up better for you in the photos, I had to cover the stain with a coat of Gesso before painting. For your painting, refer to the notes I gave you earlier about "thin" mixtures.

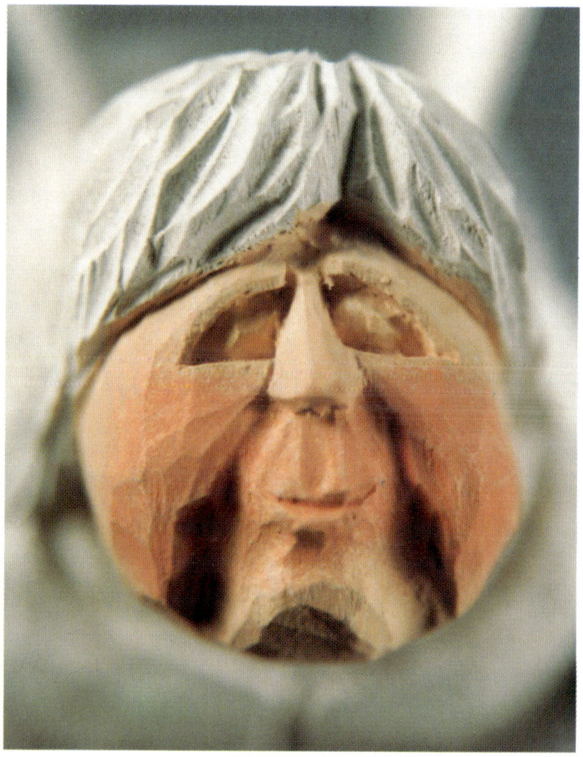

The face, hands and feet are FLESHTONE. While the face is still damp, lightly blend in a small amount of BLUSH FLESH around the mouth and cheek areas to give a slight blush to the face.

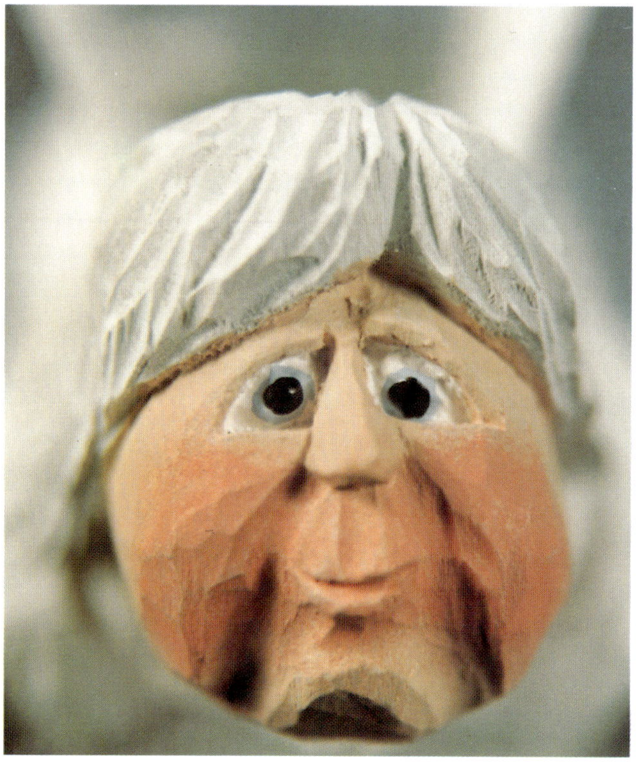

The eyes are TITANIUM WHITE. When the WHITE is dry, use a small, fine-tip brush and put a round dot of BABY BLUE in the center of the eye. When this is dry, use your fine-tip brush to put a *LAMP BLACK dot inside the BLUE dot.* The placement of the BLUE and BLACK dots will have various effects on the angel's facial expression. Experiment on a piece of scrap wood to discover all the expressions you can create. I personally like to show the eyes rolled upward, looking toward one side or the other. You may experiment with different looks and find one that you prefer also.

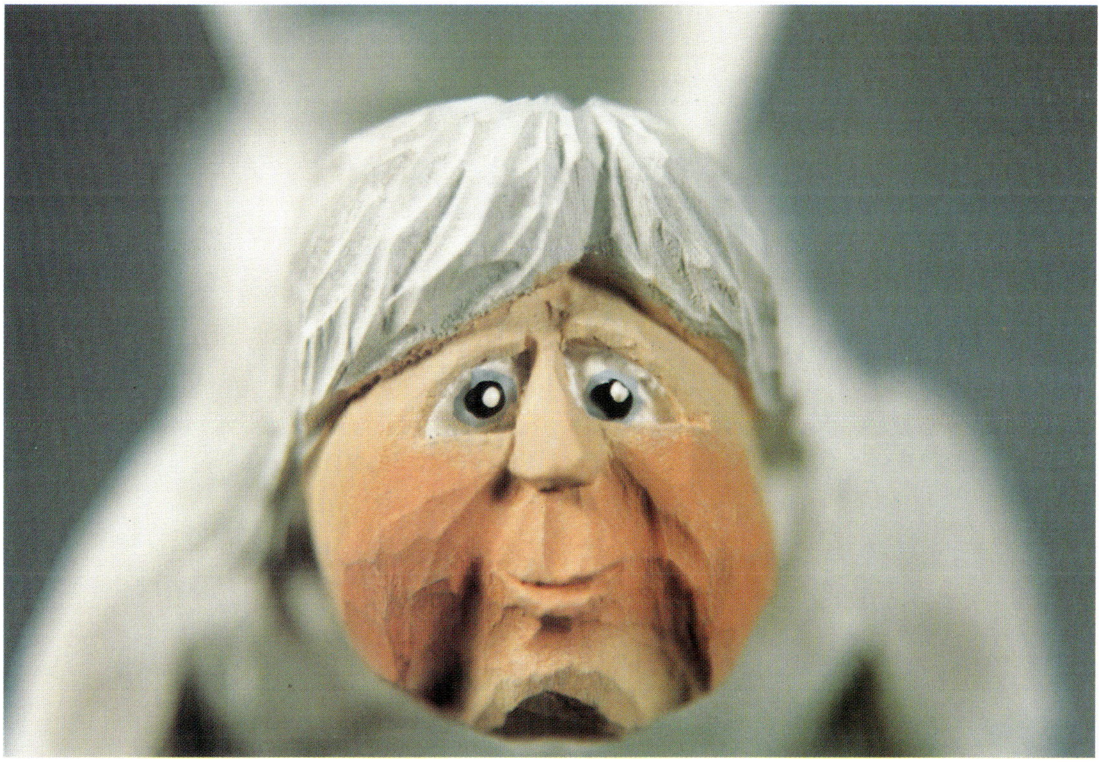

Finally, take a toothpick and put a WHITE highlight on the edge of the BLACK dot. If the eyes are looking to the left, I put the highlight around the 10 o'clock position. If looking to the right, I put the highlight around the 2 o'clock position. When looking straight ahead, you can put the highlight at either the 10 o'clock or 2 o'clock position, whichever you prefer. This is another area you can experiment with on a scrap piece of wood, to see the effects of moving the highlight around.

Paint the eyebrows using undiluted ANTIQUE GOLD. Then, using a thinned mixture of this same color, paint the hair.

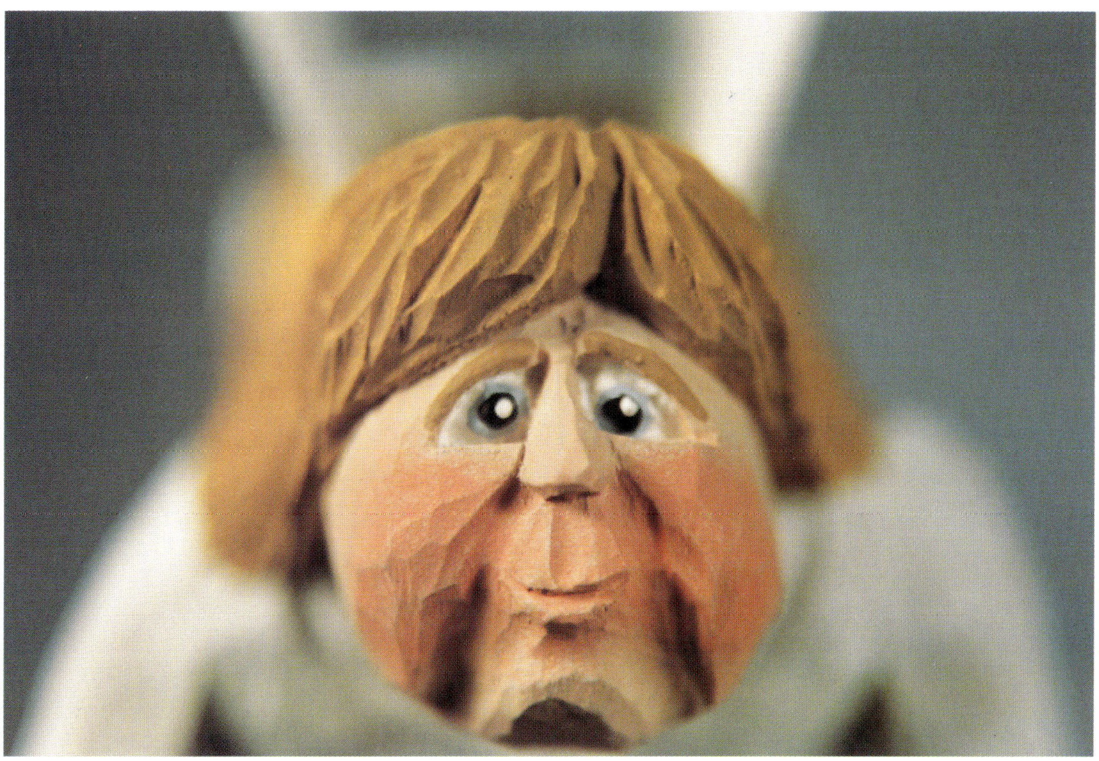

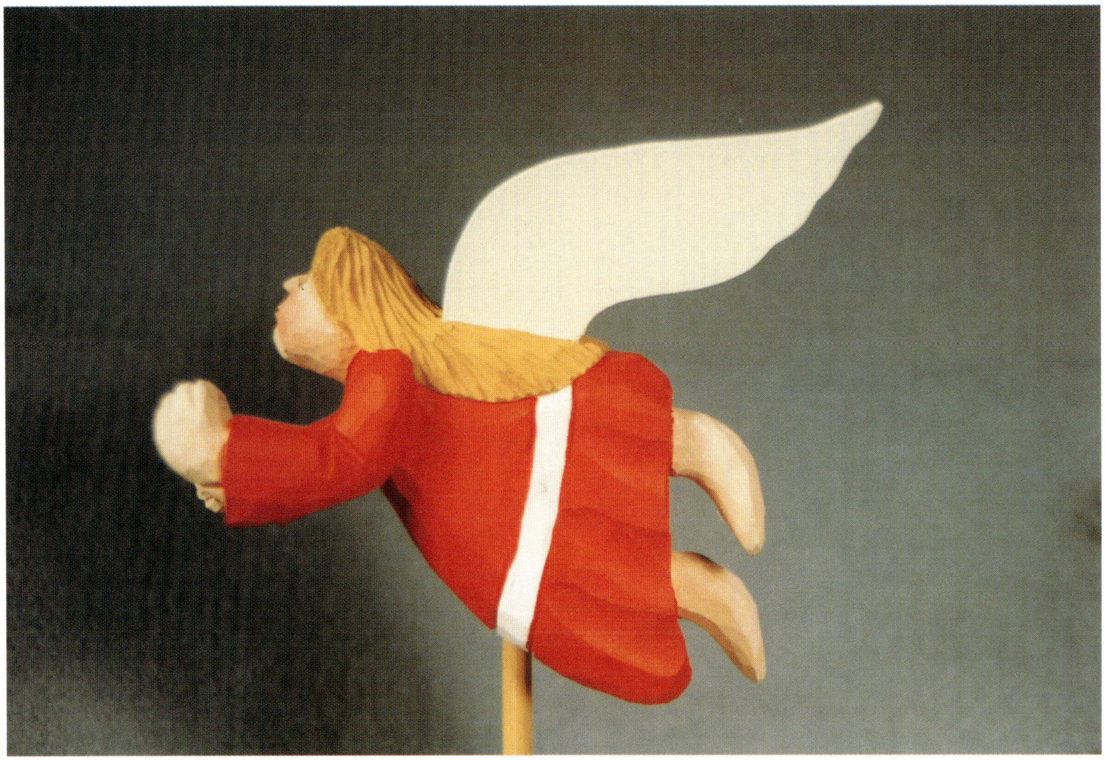

The wings are BUTTERMILK, and the robe is SANTA RED.

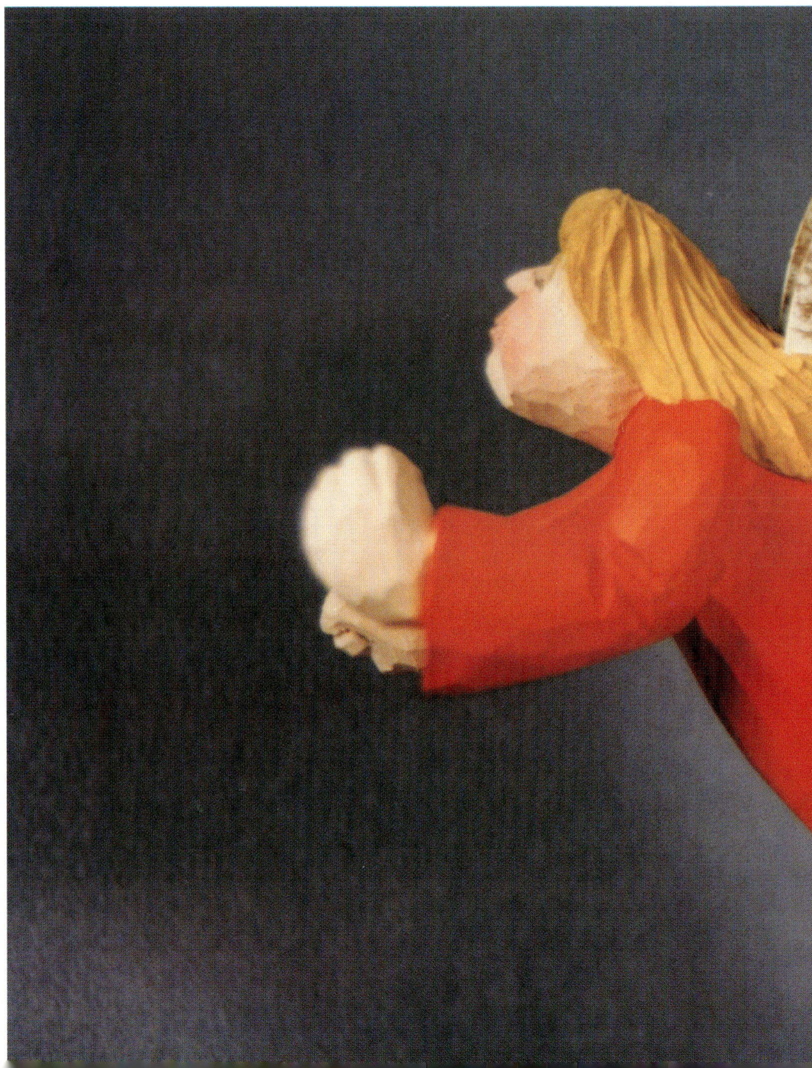

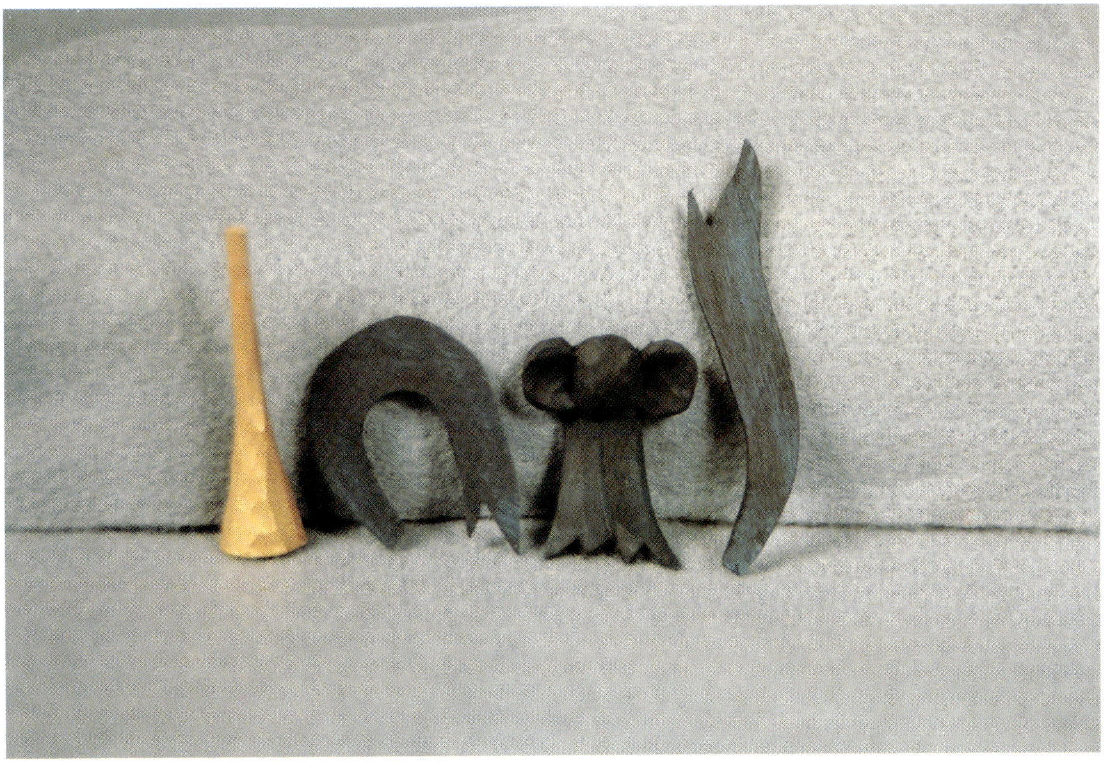

The horn is VENETIAN GOLD. The ribbon, bow, and bow sash sections on the robe are PRUSSIAN BLUE.

As an option, as shown here, you may lightly sponge Venetian Gold on both sides of the wings to add accent and give a more antique appearance.

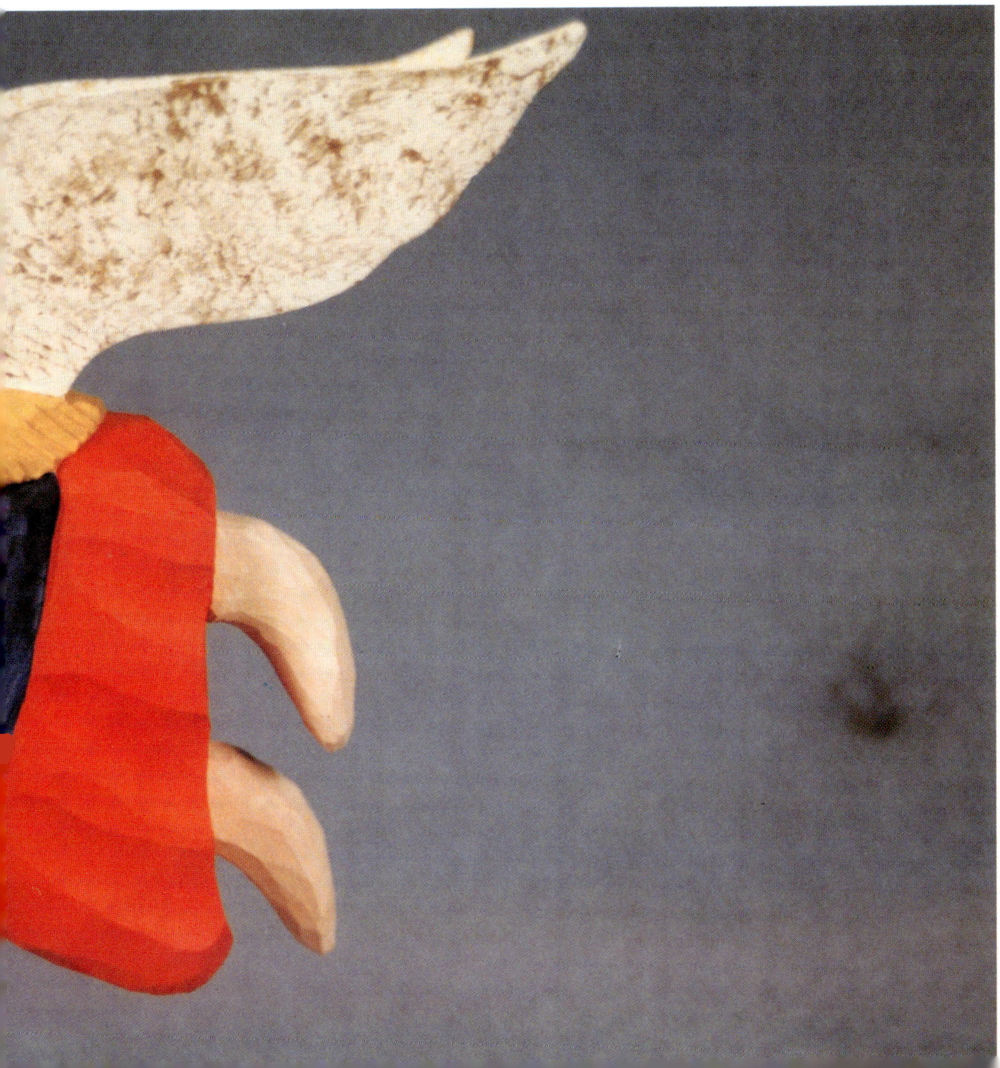

ANTIQUING & ASSEMBLING THE PROJECT

Once the paint is dry, you may want to "age" your angels with an antiquing product in order to help tone down the colors a bit. **It is easier if you do this before assembling the pieces** (bows, ribbons, horns, etc.). I have had excellent results using antiquing gels made by DecoArt. These are available at hobby and craft stores. They come in various colors, so you can create different effects.

Brush a coat of antiquing gel on the wood, then wipe it off using a damp rag or sponge. It is your option how much you wipe off. After the antiquing is dry, I like to finish my carvings with a coat of brush-on acrylic varnish. DecoArt also makes an excellent varnish. I prefer the one that leaves a Satin finish. This particular finish is not too flat nor too glossy, but leaves a "soft" look to the completed carving. **(I usually put a coat of varnish on the face, hands and other flesh areas BEFORE I antique the carving).** This will prevent these areas from absorbing too much antiquing color.

ASSEMBLING THE PROJECT

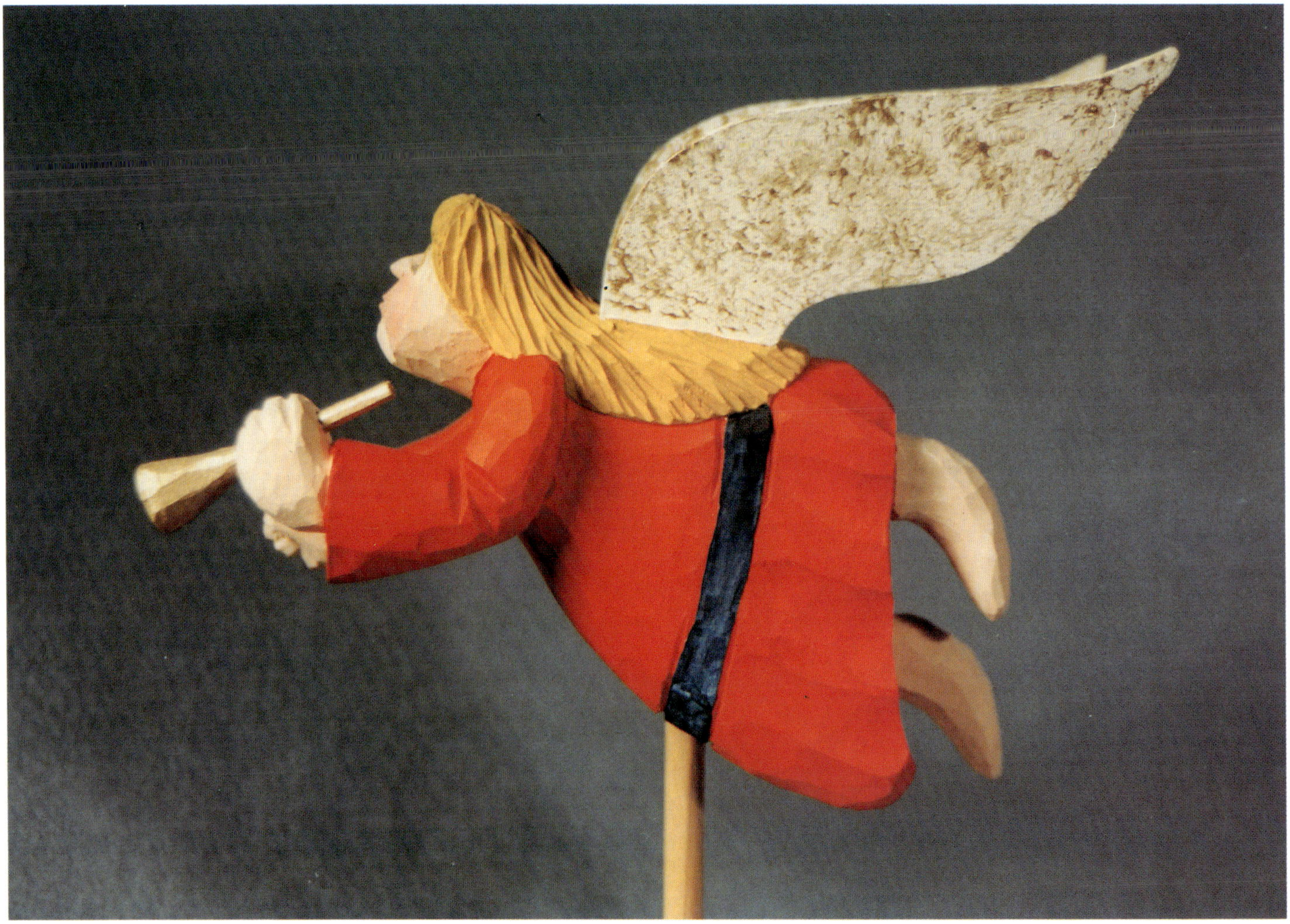

Put a small amount of glue in the hole of the left hand, and insert the horn.

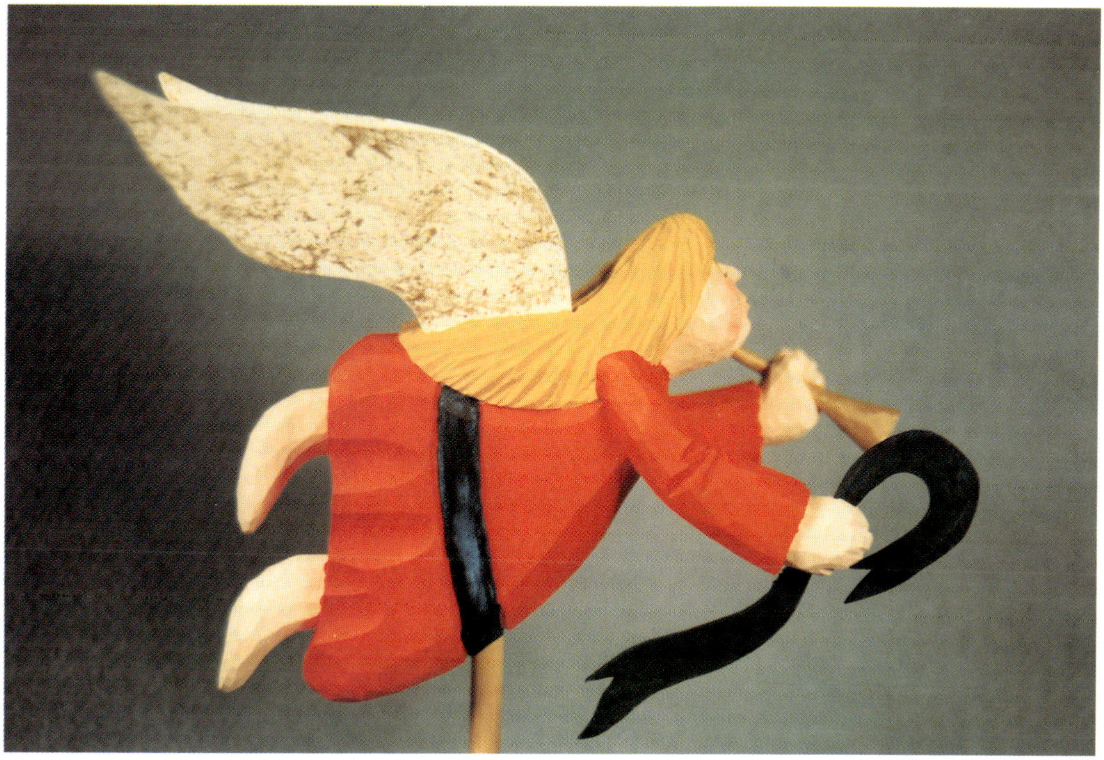

Repeat this glue procedure for the right hand and insert the ribbon sections.

The bow is glued to the side of the body where you traced it earlier. You may have to hold it in place for a minute or two until the glue sets up.

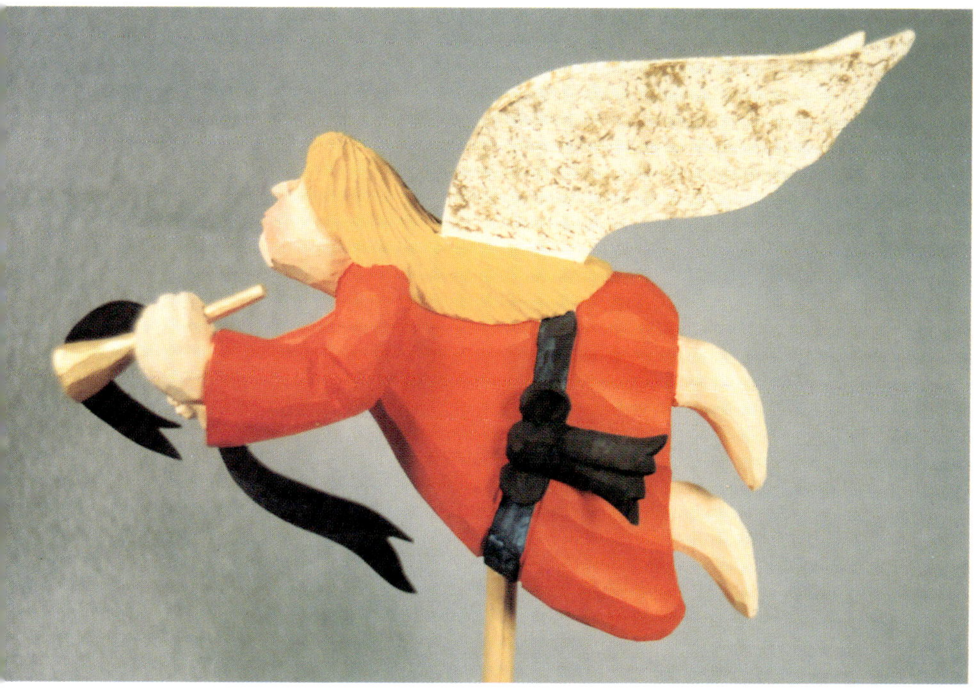

I made the base from a scrap piece of 2 x 4 lumber and a section of 5/16" diameter wooden dowel, and stained them with a Walnut color. You can mount the angel to the base at this time. (I just insert the dowel end into the body. No glue should be needed).

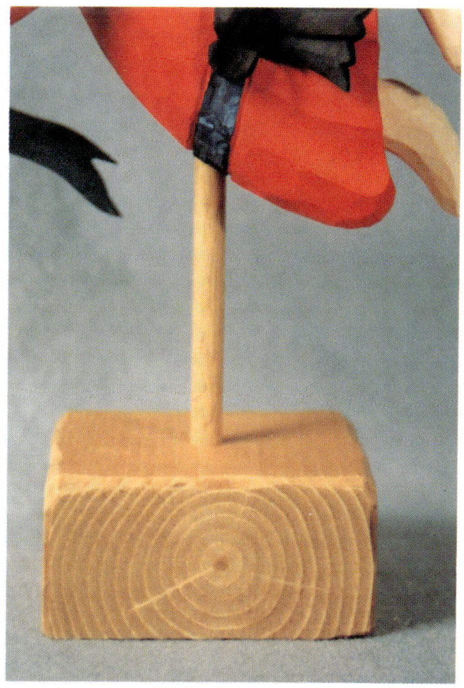

GALLERY & STUDY MODELS

When everything is dry, sign your name, and put the date on the bottom of the carving. After you become a famous carver, your signature will make your carvings more valuable. I also number my carvings, and include this number along with my signature and date. I keep a record book of sequential numbers, along with a brief description of the carving. Many times, collectors will not buy a carving unless it has a signature and a number. As your carvings become more and more "collectible", the lower numbered ones will increase in value to collectors. Your carvings are a reflection of your talent and skill... be proud of that, and put that signature on there so the whole world will know who made that masterpiece! Take a few minutes now to sit back and admire your creation.

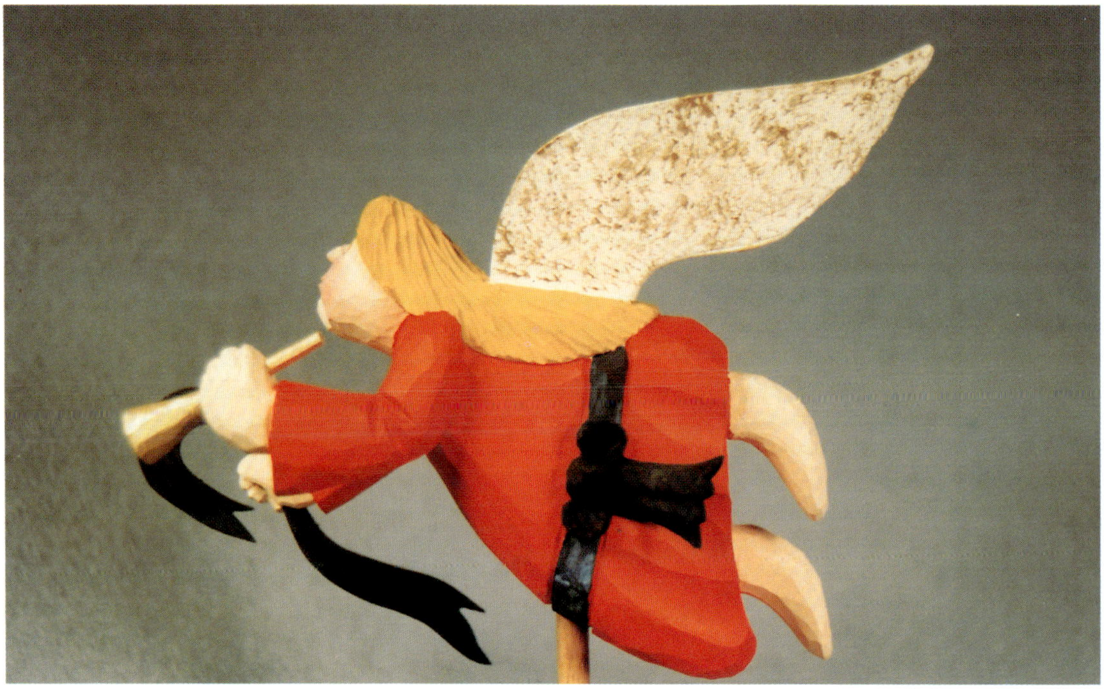

Left side view of finished project.

Right side view of finished project.

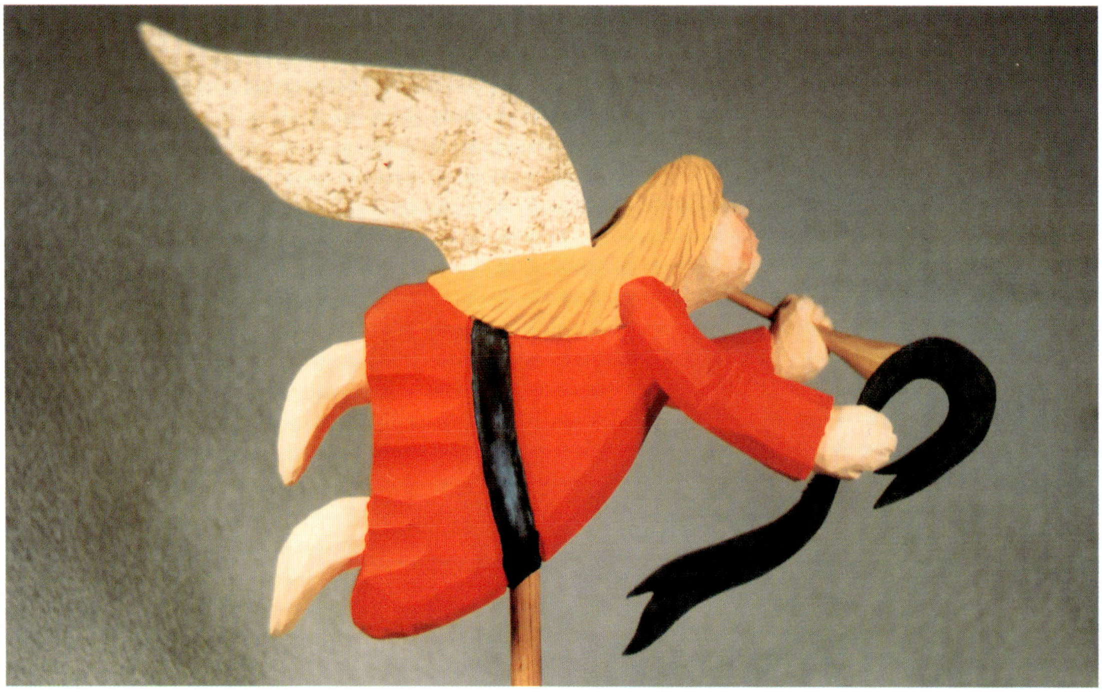

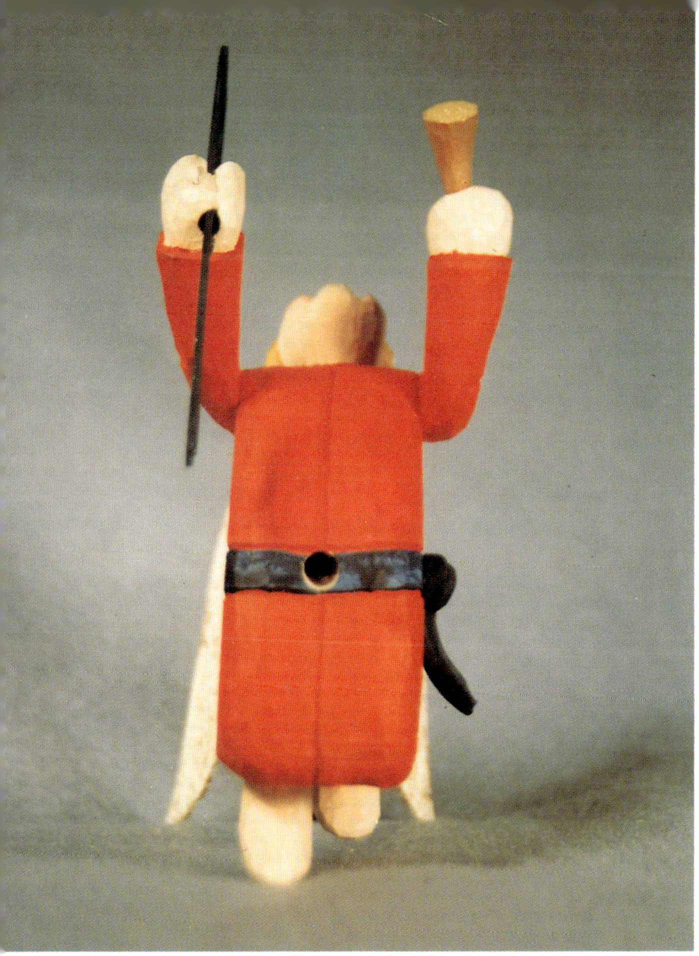

Bottom view of finished project.

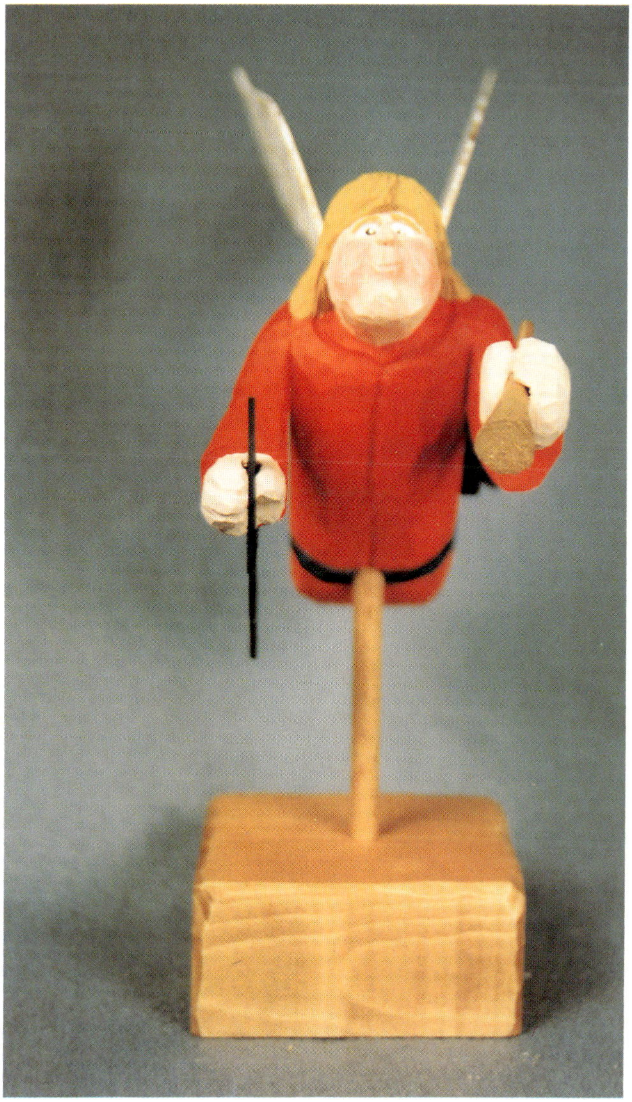

Front view of finished project.

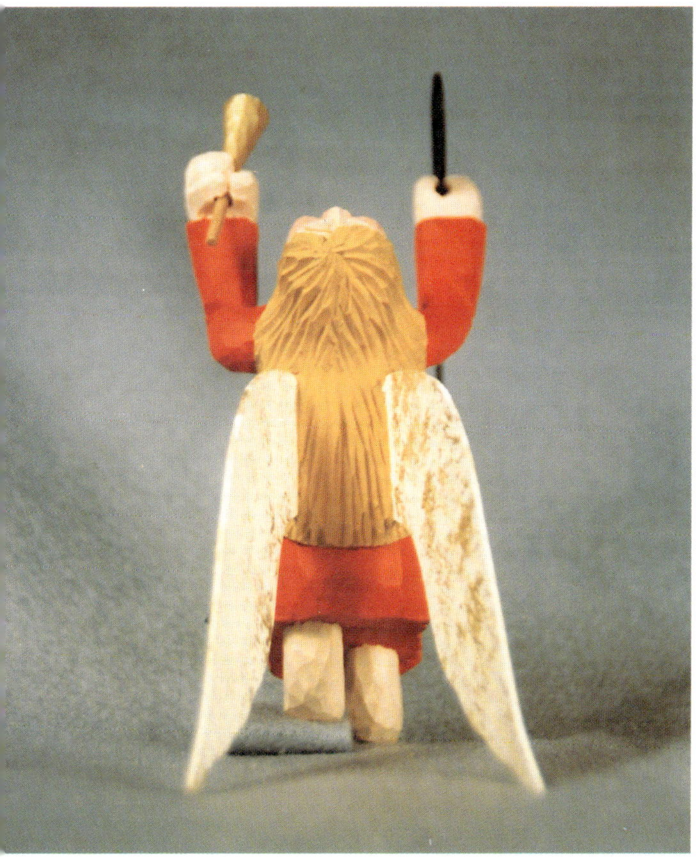

Top view of finished project

I hope that in some way I have been able to help each of you with some aspect of carving and painting. When we share tips and information, we all become better. If you have any comments or questions about something in this book, or if you have an idea you'd like to see me put in a future book, please feel free to write or call me at the following address and telephone number. I welcome any comments or suggestions you have.

Al Streetman
1609 N. Fordson Drive
Oklahoma City, OK. 73127
(405) 495-0816

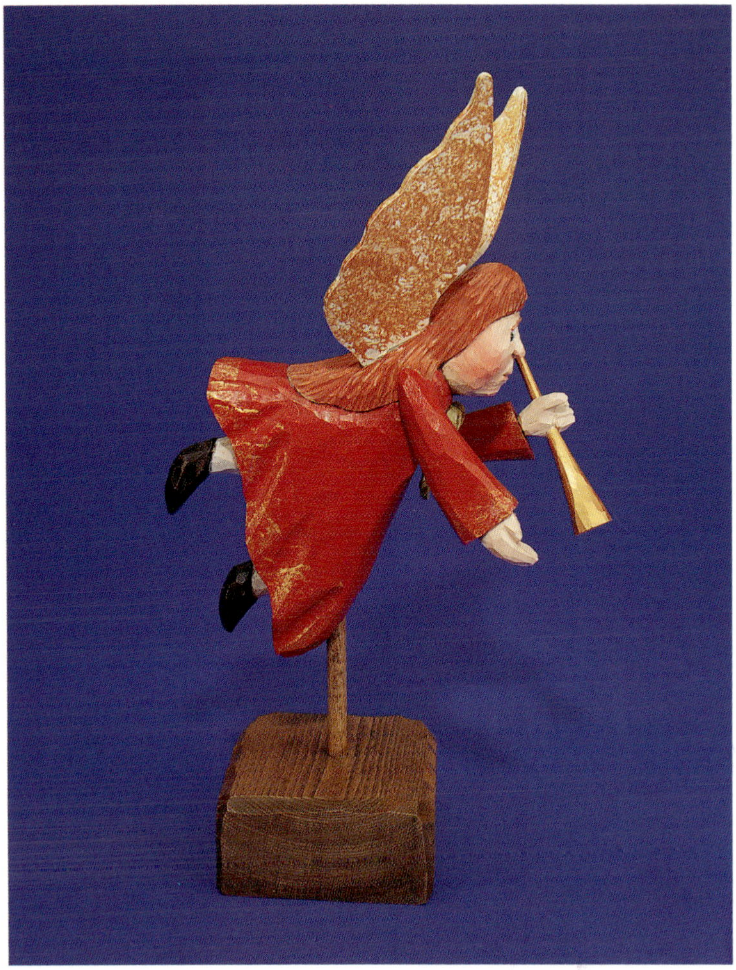

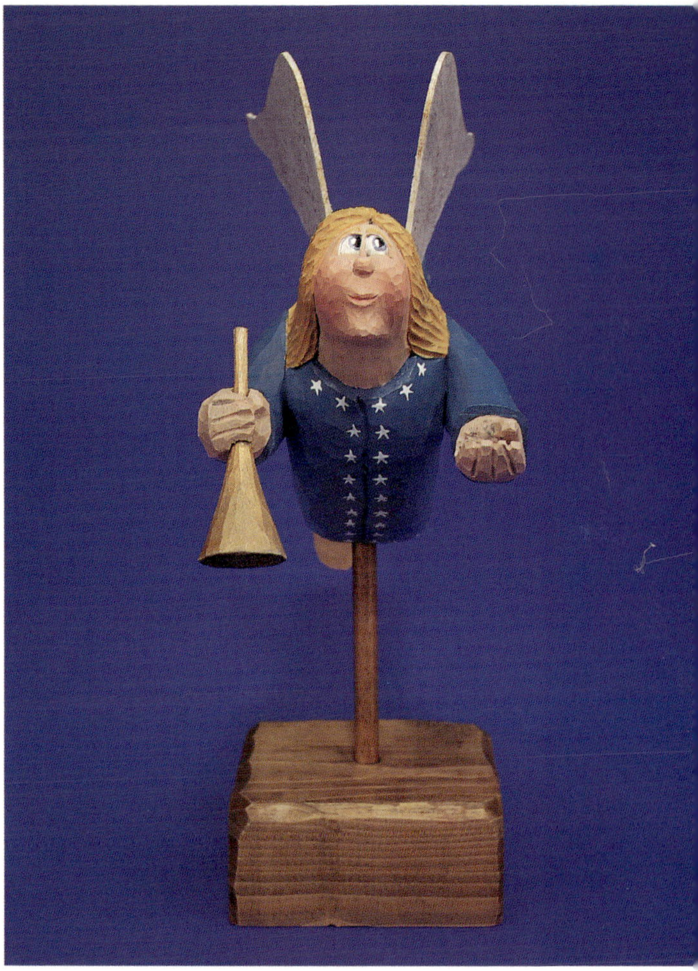

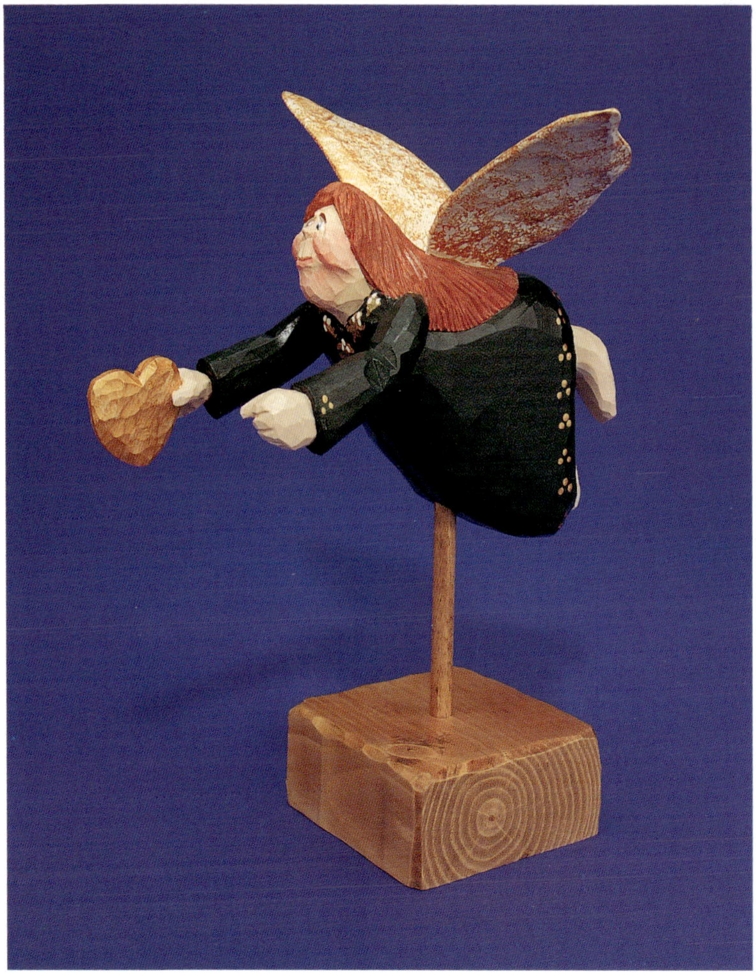